JUMPSTART! AS

This book contains a wealth of ideas for teachers to deliver engaging and informative assemblies in primary schools. The book gives a structure for any assembly that can be easily followed with minimum preparation and provides plenty of opportunities for children to learn interactively and reflect on the theme introduced.

With all the essential information on over 40 topics and complementary resources, including the author's own poetry, *Jumpstart! Assemblies* covers a variety of subjects, such as:

- personal relationships and values, including friendship, bullying, tolerance, and greed;
- health and wellbeing, including exercise, food, safety at home and online, and mental health;
- global issues, including conservation, the environment, world hunger, and peace;
- festivals and celebrations, including Diwali, Hanukkah, Ramadan, Chinese New Year, and Christmas.

This book will be an invaluable aid for any teacher who wants to jumpstart the school day with a dynamic and effective assembly.

John Foster taught English for 20 years before becoming a full-time writer. He has written over 100 books for classroom use and is a highly regarded children's poet.

Jumpstart!

JUMPSTART!
ASSEMBLIES
IDEAS AND ACTIVITIES FOR ASSEMBLIES IN PRIMARY SCHOOLS

John Foster

Routledge
Taylor & Francis Group

LONDON AND NEW YORK

First published 2019
by Routledge
2 Park Square, Milton Park, Abingdon, Oxon OX14 4RN

and by Routledge
52 Vanderbilt Avenue, New York, NY 10017

Routledge is an imprint of the Taylor & Francis Group, an informa business

© 2019 John Foster

British Library Cataloguing-in-Publication Data
A catalogue record for this book is available from the British Library

Library of Congress Cataloging-in-Publication Data
A catalog record has been requested for this book

ISBN: 978-1-138-54253-2 (hbk)
ISBN: 978-1-138-54254-9 (pbk)
ISBN: 978-1-351-00844-0 (ebk)

Typeset in Palatino and Scala Sans
by Swales & Willis Ltd, Exeter, Devon, UK

Contents

Contents

Introduction

This book contains ideas and activities for assemblies in primary schools, consisting of detailed plans on a wide range of topics. Collectively the topics covered assist schools towards meeting the aims, purposes and values of the National Curriculum by promoting the spiritual, moral, social and cultural development of primary school children. They also help to prepare them for the experiences and responsibilities that they encounter in their lives, by covering aspects of Personal, Social and Health Education.

The book is divided into four sections, according to the topics that are introduced. The first section focusses on personal relationships and values and includes assemblies on, for example, friends and friendships and bullying, as well as on values such as honesty, tolerance and manners. The second section, entitled 'Health and wellbeing', deals with emotional wellbeing, focussing on, for example, feelings of anger and sadness, and on safety issues, including internet safety, in addition to healthy eating and exercising. The third section, on global issues, is arranged around specific days which deal with environmental issues, such as conservation and pollution – Earth Day and World Oceans Day – and issues of poverty, homelessness and world peace. The final section, on festivals and celebrations, covers religious festivals, such as Eid, Guru Nanak's Birthday, Divali and Christmas, patron saints' days and other key occasions; for example, Chinese New Year and Remembrance Day.

THE UNITS

Each topic is presented separately, with the unit providing enough material for a single assembly. The units begin with a clear statement explaining what the **Aim** of the assembly is.

Where the activity requires pre-planning, there is information under the heading **Preparation** on what is necessary. In a number of units, this involves a whole class in preparing a presentation or simply typing in a few statements so that they can be displayed on the screen. There are also suggestions for appropriate pieces of music that can be played while the children are entering the assembly.

Next, there is an **Introduction**. Often, this takes the form of an explanation of the topic that is being explored, relating it to the children's experiences. This is followed by the **Main Focus**, which takes a variety of forms according to the topic; for example, a PowerPoint presentation, a poem or a story, or a presentation by a particular class. Every opportunity is taken to involve the children in the activities; for example, by asking them questions or asking them to vote on an issue. Finally, there is a **Conclusion** suggesting how the assembly can be ended.

A unique feature of the book is that many of the units contain a poem that deals with an aspect of the topic. There are also suggestions for songs that can be incorporated into the assembly.

Many units conclude with an appropriate prayer. The prayers are drawn from different religions. The units also have a section entitled **Thought for the day** which contains statements on the topic, such as proverbs from different cultures and relevant quotations by famous people. These can be prominently displayed around the school.

Finally, there are details of **Further resources**, including links to useful websites.

CHAPTER 1

Personal relationships and values

BULLYING

Each year there is an Anti-Bullying Week. This assembly can form part of a school's focus on bullying during Anti-Bullying Week.

Aim
To understand what it feels like to be bullied and that there are different types of bullying, and to explore ways of dealing with bullying.

Preparation
Obtain photos of Batman, Kate Winslet, Tiger Woods and Justin Timberlake from the internet to put on the screen.

Two songs which you could prepare for the children to listen to and sing during the assembly are 'Mean' by Taylor Swift and 'Beautiful' by Christina Aguilera.

Introduction
Read the poem 'Four O'clock Friday'.

Four O'clock Friday
> Four o'clock Friday, I'm home at last.
> Time to forget the week that's past.
> On Monday, in break they stole my ball
> And threw it over the playground wall.
> On Tuesday afternoon, in games
> They threw mud at me and called me names.

On Wednesday, they trampled my books on the floor,
So Miss kept me in because I swore.
On Thursday, they laughed after the test
'Cause my marks were lower than the rest.
Four o'clock Friday, at last I'm free,
For two whole days they can't get at me.

Ask: How does the person in the poem feel? How does it feel to be bullied? Then put the four photographs on the board and ask: What do these four people have in common? Answer: They were all bullied at school.

Justin Timberlake was called a sissy because he didn't like sports, and bullies made fun of his love of acting.

Batman star Christian Bale was punched and kicked.

Golfer Tiger Woods was picked on and racially abused.

Actress Kate Winslet was bullied because of her appearance. She was called 'Blubber' and was locked in a cupboard.

Main focus

Point out that there are different types of bullying: mental and physical. Mental bullying includes name-calling, ignoring and excluding someone, threatening them and putting hurtful comments about them on social media.

Read the scenario 'Gemma's story' and ask: What should Gemma do? Should she try to deal with the situation herself? Should she talk to an adult? If so, should she talk to a teacher or her parents?

Gemma's story
Gemma was happy at her old school and had lots of friends. But when the family moved because her mum got a new job, Gemma had to go to a new school. The girls in her new class

ignored her and made fun of her accent. One girl in particular picked on her and called her Posh. The girl saw that this upset Gemma so she posted spiteful messages about Gemma anonymously on social media.

Conclusion

List their suggestions about what they think Gemma should do on the screen. Encourage them to add to the list by asking: What is the best way to deal with bullies? Stress that involving an adult is better than getting into a fight and that it is not telling tales to do so, because everyone has the right not to be bullied.

End with this short prayer:

Let us remember that when we poke fun at someone they may feel pain.
Let us remember that when we pick on someone they feel angry and afraid.
Let us remember that when we see someone being bullied they are alone.
Give us the courage to confront the bullies and to comfort and befriend those who are being bullied.

Thoughts for the day

Sticks and stones can break my bones, but words can never hurt me.

Traditional saying

Each of us deserves the freedom to pursue our own version of happiness. No one deserves to be bullied.

Barack Obama

Do not be a bystander. If you see something, say something.

Manwar Khan

Follow-up activity

Encourage the children to do the Bullying Dilemmas quiz from the Kidscape website.

3

FRIENDS AND FRIENDSHIPS

Aim
To think about what makes a person a good friend and how you expect friends to behave towards each other.

Preparation
As preparation for the assembly, classes can play a version of the Friendship Game by making a board with 36 squares on it and putting details of positive behaviour that will cement a friendship (e.g. *You agree to do what your friend wants, even though you'd prefer to do something else*) on eight randomly chosen squares and details of negative behaviour (e.g. *You make jokes about your friend behind their back*) on eight randomly chosen squares. Two or more people can play the game, taking it in turns to throw a dice. If they land on a positive statement they go forward two spaces. If they land on a negative space they go back two spaces. The person who reaches the finish first is the winner. After they have played the game, hold a discussion about what they learned from the game about how to behave towards friends.

Download the song 'The Friendship Shuffle' from www.songspun. com.

Other songs you can prepare for the children to listen to and sing include 'You've Got a Friend in Me' by Randy Newman and 'You've Got a Friend' by Carole King.

Ask one of the classes to prepare a reading of the poem 'A Friend Is . . .'

Introduction
Ask the children each to think about how they behave towards a friend. What kinds of behaviour are likely to help a friendship to develop? What kinds of behaviour are likely to damage a friendship?

Write these two headings on the board and build up two lists like the ones below:

Ways to behave with a friend	Ways of behaving that will harm a friendship
Comfort them when they feel sad	Telling tales behind their backs
Sharing things with them	Borrowing things and not giving them back
Doing something they want to do	Always wanting your own way
Sticking up for them	Lying to them
Listening to their point of view	Expecting them always to agree with you

When you have completed the lists, ask the children to decide which ways of behaving they think are the most important in helping to make friendships, and to say what they think is the most important of all.

Main focus: How should friends behave?
Read this poem:

I Told My Friend a Secret
>I told my friend a secret.
>She promised not to tell.
>My friend told her friend.
>She told her friend as well.
>
>Now everyone knows my secret.
>I think that it's unfair.
>I told my friend I trusted her.
>That's why I pulled her hair.

Talk about the two children and how they behaved. Who do they think behaved worse – the girl who didn't keep the secret or the girl who pulled her friend's hair? How could the girl who pulled her friend's hair have reacted differently?

Discuss keeping secrets. Is it always right to promise to keep a secret? What if keeping the secret will endanger your friend in some way? Are there some occasions in which you should break your promise?

Put up the poem 'A Friend Is . . .' on the board and ask a class which has prepared a reading of it to present their reading.

A Friend Is . . .

A friend is someone you can rely on
A shoulder to cry on
A friend is someone who cares.
A friend is someone who shares.

A friend is someone who won't let you down
Someone who sticks by your side
A friend is someone who listens to you
And in whom you can confide.

A friend is someone who won't force you
To do things you don't want to do
A friend is someone who will always
Keep their promises to you.

A friend is someone you can trust
A friend is loyal and true
Someone you can depend on
Who is always there for you.

Conclusion
Play the song 'The Friendship Shuffle', encouraging everyone to join in by putting the words up on the screen.

End with the thoughts for the day.

Thoughts for the day
Don't walk in front of me . . . I may not follow. Don't walk behind me . . . I may not lead. Walk beside me . . . just be my friend.

Albert Camus

Do unto others as you would have them do unto you.

English proverb

GREED

Aim
To consider what the consequences of being greedy can be and why we shouldn't be greedy.

Preparation
Two songs which you could prepare for the children to listen to and sing are 'I Want It All' by Queen and 'Gold Digger' by Kanye West ft. Jamie Foxx.

Type the list of statements about the story of King Midas into the computer so that you can put them on the screen (see below).

Introduction
Ask the children to think of a time when they acted greedily. How did they feel afterwards? Ashamed? Guilty? Pleased? Sorry? Embarrassed? Happy? Invite some of them to share their memories of being greedy and how they felt.

Ask: What do you think other people thought of you when you acted greedily? Do you think it affected what they thought of you?

Main focus: The effects of being greedy
Read the story 'The Golden Touch'.

The Golden Touch

King Midas had a beautiful daughter with long golden hair who was called Marigold, whom he loved very much.

He was very rich. So rich that one of the rooms in his palace was full of gold.

King Midas loved his gold. He loved it as much as he loved his daughter.

Although he was very rich, King Midas was greedy. He dreamed of being the richest person in the world.

One night he was woken by a noise in his room. At the foot of his bed stood a boy, dressed in a gold cloak. In his hand, he was holding a golden wand.

'Midas,' he said. 'Is it true that you love gold and want to be the richest man in the world?'

King Midas nodded.

'If you had one wish would it be to have as much gold as you wanted?'

'My wish would be that everything I touched would turn to gold.'

'In the morning, you shall have your wish,' said the boy. In his hand the golden wand glowed and the boy vanished.

The next day, King Midas was up and dressed before dawn. He was eager to see if what the boy said would come true.

He was in the palace garden when the sun rose. He reached out to pick a flower and it turned to gold at his touch.

He rushed indoors and began to go round the great hall of the palace. He picked up a china dish and it turned to gold. He ran round the room touching things. They all turned to gold, even the curtains and the pictures on the wall.

'I am now the richest man in the world,' he shouted. Just then, his daughter came into the room.

'What's going on?' she asked. When King Midas saw her, he rushed towards her to hug her and tell her the good news.

But when he touched her, she turned into a gold statue.

King Midas let go of her and stared. Suddenly, he felt afraid. What had he done?

He looked at all the gold around him. What use was it to him? He would give it all away, if only he could get his daughter back.

There was a flash of light and the boy stood before him again.

'Do you still want to be the richest man in the world?' he asked.

King Midas shook his head. 'No!' he cried.

'Then take this wand,' said the boy. He held out a plain wooden wand. 'Touch all the things you turned to gold with this wand and they will become as they were before.'

King Midas took the wand. The first thing he touched was the statue. His daughter stood before him again. Then he went round touching all the other things he had turned to gold.

And from that day, King Midas set about emptying his room that was full of gold. He used some of it to give to the poor. Some of it he used to build houses, schools and hospitals. He became known for his generosity and his kingdom flourished as his gold touched many lives.

Talk about the message of the story. Ask: What is the moral of the story? What do you think of the way King Midas behaves? What sort of person is he? How would you describe him?

Put the list of statements below on the white board. Focus on each statement in turn and ask the children to put up their hands to indicate whether they agree with it.

- King Midas was a foolish man.
- The boy with the wand taught King Midas a lesson.
- Most people would behave as King Midas did.
- King Midas is a clever man.
- The message of the story is 'Gold is the most important thing in the world.'
- King Midas is selfish and greedy.
- The moral of the story is 'Your family is more valuable than how rich you are.'

Conclusion

End with the prayer below and a joke.

> Lord, help us to avoid being greedy and selfish.
> Help us to understand that we should not be envious of what other people have.
> Help us to understand that we should not want to have more than our fair share.
> Help us to be unselfish in all that we do.

Joke of the day

What's the difference between a hungry person and a greedy one? A hungry person longs to eat and a greedy person eats too long.

Thoughts for the day

If more of us valued food and cheer and song above hoarded gold, the world would be a merrier place.

J.R.R. Tolkien

Earth provides enough to satisfy every man's need, but not every man's greed.

Mahatma Gandhi

HEROES

Aim

To think about people they admire and why they admire them and about who they think are heroes.

Preparation

You could prepare David Bowie's song 'Heroes' to listen to and sing at the end of the assembly.

Ask each class to prepare for this assembly by choosing a person they consider to be a hero and to nominate the person for election to a Hall of Fame. When they have decided whom they are going to nominate, ask each class to choose a spokesperson to explain the reasons why that person should be in the Hall of Fame.

Prepare a ballot box for each class and ballot papers on which are the names of the people who are nominated.

Put the name of each spokesperson on a piece of paper and draw lots to decide the order in which they will speak.

Introduction

Explain that the assembly is going to take the form of a debate about who they admire and who they would choose to elect to a Hall of Fame. The spokesperson from each class will say why they have chosen to nominate their candidate. Then the debate will continue with anyone else saying why they think a particular person should be chosen. Finally a vote will be taken.

Main focus: Who do you regard as a hero?

Hold the debate, then organise a secret ballot. Ask the class teachers to hand out the ballot papers. Each child can vote for only one person by putting a cross against the name of the person they would select. (Note: You can prevent the children from just voting for the person their class nominated by asking the class teacher to cross out that name on their class's ballot papers.)

Appoint two teachers to count the ballots. While they are doing so, talk about people who we regard as heroes. Often we admire them because of their talents and achievements. They include sports stars, such as footballers; film and TV actors; and pop stars.

Present the results of the debate and discuss what the results tell you about the people who are regarded as heroes.

Conclusion

End the assembly by talking about unsung heroes – ordinary people who act unselfishly by caring for family members who are ill or disabled. And people such as volunteer fire officers, who risk their lives to save others. Also, people who unselfishly give up their time voluntarily to help others. Ask them to think of people they know who could be considered unsung heroes.

Read them what Joanne said when she was asked to think about unsung heroes:

> My Uncle Trevor is an unsung hero. He's a volunteer fire fighter. He's prepared to risk his life by going into burning buildings to rescue people.

Thought for the day

> I think a hero is any person really intent on making this a better place for all people.
>
> Maya Angelou

11

HONESTY

Aim
To explore what honesty means and the potential consequences of not behaving honestly and not telling the truth.

Preparation
Choose four upper juniors to be hotseated as 'Thomas', 'Jessica', 'Dwayne' and 'Lester', who appear in the scenario 'The Watch', which forms the main focus of the assembly. Give them each a copy of the story and make sure they understand their character's view of what to do with the watch.

Songs which you could prepare for the children to listen to at the start or end of the assembly are: 'Honesty' by Billy Joel; 'Honest' by The Chainsmokers; 'Would I Lie to You?' by Eurythmics.

Introduction
Begin by getting the children to think about what being honest means. It means telling the truth. It means owning up. It means not stealing. It means not lying.

Read this poem:

I Told a Lie
> I told a lie. It haunts me still.
> They looked sad because they knew
> That I was responsible
> Though I said it was you.
>
> I told a lie. It weighs me down.
> I let you take the blame.
> And now you do not trust me
> And all I feel is shame.

Ask: What does this poem tell us about the consequences of telling a lie and how a person who tells a lie may feel?

Main focus: Making honest decisions

Scenario: The Watch

> Lester was playing in the park one day when he found a watch. It was an expensive-looking watch and it was much better than the cheap watch that Lester had. He was thinking about what he should do with it when a group of his friends came along. He showed them the watch and they began to discuss what he should do with it.
>
> 'You found it, so it's yours. I'd keep it if I were you,' said Thomas.
>
> 'You should hand it in to the police,' said Jessica.
>
> They started to argue. 'What if it's stolen?' said Lester.
>
> 'You'd be stealing it if you keep it,' said Jessica.
>
> 'You could sell it,' said Dwayne. 'That's what I'd do.'
>
> 'What if it belonged to someone who will be very upset because it's special in some way?' said Jessica.
>
> 'They shouldn't have been so careless as to lose it then,' said Thomas. 'If it was me, I'd keep it.'

Read the story. Then ask the three individuals you have chosen to role-play Thomas, Jessica and Dwayne to explain what they would do, giving their reasons. Then ask them what they think the consequences would be of them (a) keeping it, (b) selling it, and (c) handing it in.

Ask some people in the audience to suggest who the watch might belong to and how they would feel about losing it.

Finally, ask the person chosen to be Lester what he would do. Would his decision be different if he knew who the watch belonged to?

Conclusion

End with this prayer and/or a thought for today.

> Dear God
> Help us to be honest and to own up when we have done something wrong.

Help us not to lie and not to blame others for our mistakes.
Help us always to tell the truth.
Help us to say sorry when our actions are hurtful.

Thoughts for the day

Being honest may not get you a lot of friends. But it will always get you the right ones.

John Lennon

If it's not right, don't do it. If it's not true, don't say it.

Marcus Aurelius

If you want to be trusted, be honest. If you want to be honest, be true.

Unknown

LITTER

Aim

To understand the reasons why we shouldn't drop litter.

Preparation

Collect a range of examples of litter, including a newspaper, plastic bottle, piece of cardboard, milk carton, disposable nappy, piece of orange peel, glass bottle, paper towel and cigarette butt. Put all the items in a black plastic bin bag.

Download a PowerPoint presentation about litter, e.g. from the Eco Schools website.

Prepare to show videos of Mr Eco's 'Litterbug' song and 'The Litterbug with Lyrics' song from YouTube.

Two other songs you can prepare to incorporate into the assembly are: 'Litter Rap' and 'I Love Trash', both from *Sesame Street*.

Invite a class to learn and to work out a presentation of the poem 'The Litter-Lout Twins'. They could include role-plays explaining why littering is not only unsightly but can spread diseases and harm animals.

The Litter-Lout Twins
>Lennie and Laura,
>The litter-lout twins,
>Always drop rubbish,
>Never use bins.
>
>Chuck empty crisp packets
>Up in the air.
>Lennie and Laura,
>They don't care.
>
>Toss empty drink cans
>Onto the ground,
>Throw away sweet wrappers
>Let them blow around.
>
>Go for a picnic,
>Scatter rubbish everywhere.
>Lennie and Laura,
>They don't care.
>
>Lennie gives Laura
>Some gum to chew.
>She spits it on the pavement
>Where it sticks to your shoe.
>
>Lennie and Laura,
>The litter-lout twins,
>Always drop rubbish,
>Never use bins.

Introduction

Explain that this week is Anti-Litter Week, organised by Keep Britain Tidy, and begin by emptying the contents of your bin onto a table. Ask a number of individuals: How many items of litter do you think are dropped each day in Britain? The answer is an estimated two and a quarter million.

Ask: Why does this matter? First, it is unsightly – point to the mess that you have put on the table. Second, it damages the environment and can harm animals.

Hold up the items from the table one by one and ask: How long do you think it will take for each of these items to decompose?

Put the list of correct answers up on the screen.

- Paper towel: 2–4 weeks
- Newspaper: 6 weeks
- Cardboard: 2 months
- Orange peel: 6 months
- Milk carton: 5 years
- Cigarette butt: 10–12 years
- Plastic bottle: 450 years
- Aluminium can: 500 years
- Disposable nappy: 550 years
- Glass bottle: NEVER

Main focus: The reasons why we shouldn't drop litter

Invite the class to give their presentation and afterwards ask them what they have learned from preparing it about the problem of litter.

Show the PowerPoint which you downloaded.

Points to stress are:

1. It is up to everybody to keep the neighbourhood clean and tidy. If you drop litter you show a lack of respect for everyone who lives there.
2. Litter attracts rats and flies, which can spread diseases.
3. Litter can harm pets and farm animals if they eat plastic or step on broken glass.
4. Litter pollutes the sea.
5. Cleaning up litter costs local councils thousands of pounds which could be spent elsewhere, e.g. on filling in potholes.

Show the video of Mr Eco's 'Litterbug' song. Then show the video of 'Litterbug' with accompanying lyrics and get the children to join in and sing the song.

Conclusion

End with some anti-litter slogans:

Stop it! Don't drop it!

Make every day an anti-litter day.

When you see a bin, put your litter in.

Challenge the children to think up their own anti-litter slogans to put up round the school.

Thought for the day

Litter is disgusting. So are the people who drop it.

MANNERS

Aim

To understand the importance of good manners.

Preparation

Encourage an infant or lower junior class to prepare a list of what are considered to be good manners in British society. They could prepare a number of posters which they present as 'The Good Manners Guide'.

Invite one of the upper junior classes to prepare a number of sketches in which they act out scenes which show children behaving in a bad-mannered way, then being reprimanded by someone who explains why such behaviour is considered bad manners.

Introduction

Start with these two jokes:

- Why are sausages rude? Because they spit at you when you cook them!
- What did the alien say to the petrol pump? 'Don't pick your nose when I'm talking to you!'

Talk about why spitting and picking your nose are bad manners, and explain that the theme of the assembly is manners.

Main focus: What are good manners? What are bad manners?

Explain that manners – how you behave – are often a matter of custom. Different societies have different views about manners, and what are considered to be good manners in one country may be considered to be bad manners in another country. Ask the children if they know of any examples. Then give them examples from this list:

- In many countries, it is the custom to take off your shoes when entering someone's home.
- In China, belching is considered a way of showing appreciation for the food you have been given.
- In many Arab countries, your left hand should not be used for eating because it is regarded as unclean.
- In Japan, blowing your nose in a handkerchief is regarded as bad manners.
- In India, if you clear your plate, your host will fill it with more food because they will think you are still hungry.
- In some countries, making the 'OK' sign with thumb and forefinger is a rude gesture.

Then ask members of the class who made the list of good manners to present the list. Make sure that the list includes the following:

- Saying 'Please' and 'Thank you'.
- Saying 'Sorry', e.g. if you bump into someone or block their way.
- Saying 'Excuse me', e.g. if someone is blocking your way.
- Greeting someone by saying 'Good morning' and 'How are you?'
- Smiling when you greet someone you haven't met before, and shaking their hand.
- Covering your face and mouth if you cough or sneeze.
- Waiting your turn in a queue.

- Holding a door open either to let someone go through it before you or to stop it from hitting them as it swings back.
- Keeping your distance and not invading another person's personal space.

Invite the upper junior class to perform their sketches.

Conclusion
End the assembly by asking the members of the class to explain what they have learned about good manners from their sketches.

Thoughts for the day
Show others the respect that you expect them to show you and always behave in the way that you expect them to behave.

Erica Stewart

No one has ever been offended by someone with good manners.

Vikrat Parsai

PERSEVERANCE

Aim
To communicate the value of perseverance.

Preparation
Choose a class to prepare a performance of the poem 'We Have the Power'.

You could prepare one or more of these songs for them to include in their performance: 'We Are the Champions' by Queen; 'Hall of Fame' by The Script; 'Wavin' Flag' by K'Naan; 'Don't Stop Believing' by Journey.

We Have the Power
We can climb mountains.
We can sail across seas.
We can cross deserts.
We can do as we please.

(Chorus)
For we have the power
The power that we need
The power to achieve
The power to succeed.

We can fly rockets.
We can reach for the stars.
We can journey to Jupiter,
Saturn and Mars.

(Chorus)

We can build robots.
We can find the solution
To the problems of hunger
And waste and pollution.

(Chorus)

We can make a world
That is equal and fair
A world in which everyone
Knows how to share.

(Chorus)

Introduction

Introduce the theme of the assembly by asking: Do you know what perseverance is? Hear some of the children's responses. Then provide this definition of perseverance: the determination to continue doing something in order to achieve success in spite of any difficulties.

Main focus: The value of perseverance

Tell the children the story of Thomas Edison, who was an American inventor, famous for inventing the light bulb. During his life he had several other groundbreaking inventions. As well as the light bulb he invented the phonograph and the alkaline battery. Throughout his career he took out patents on over 1,000 inventions. But most of his inventions were unsuccessful. This did not deter him. He kept on trying to invent things and was single-minded in his determination.

Edison believed that success is 1% inspiration and 99% perspiration. He said: 'The three things that are most essential to success are common sense, hard work and stick-to-it-iv-ness.'

He also said: 'Our greatest weakness lies in giving up. The most certain way to succeed is to try just one more time.'

Talk about how everyone has the power within themselves to keep going at a task and to succeed. Invite the class to present their performance of 'We Have the Power'.

Conclusion
End by singing the song.

Thoughts for the day
If at first you don't succeed, try and try again.

Proverb

Perseverance is failing 19 times and succeeding the 20th.

Julie Andrews

But as for you, be strong and do not give up, for your work will be rewarded.

The Bible, 2 Chronicles 15:7

Some succeed because they are destined to. Most succeed because they are determined.

Henry Van Dyke

RIGHT AND WRONG

Aim
To understand the difference between right and wrong behaviour.

Preparation

Invite a class to prepare for the assembly by making placards about what they think are right and wrong ways of behaving. For example, placards about right behaviour would include statements such as 'Tell the truth', 'Respect other people's property' and 'Respect people's religious beliefs'. Statements about wrong behaviours would include 'Vandalising', 'Lying', 'Fighting', 'Swearing', 'Bullying', 'Cheating' and 'Spitting'.

Introduction

Introduce the theme of the assembly by asking the children to think of how we consider certain ways of behaving as right and certain ways of behaving as wrong.

Main focus: What is right? What is wrong?

Ask the class who have prepared the placards to present them with those holding right ways standing at one side of the room and those holding wrong ways on the other side of the room.

Ask the children in the audience to suggest any other ways of behaving that they can think of which are either right or wrong.

Scenario: Jack's story

Jack didn't know what to do. His parents had taught him to be honest and to tell the truth. But he was afraid of the consequences if he told anyone what he had seen. Miss Henshaw, their class teacher, had sent him to the secretary's office to deliver a message. On the way back to their classroom he had seen Nathan Jennings in the cloakroom. Nathan was going through the pockets of a jacket. He was so intent on what he was doing that he didn't see Jack go by.

Jack's mind was in a whirl. There had been a number of thefts from the cloakroom recently. What should he do? If he told Miss Henshaw he would be labelled a sneak. There was an unwritten rule that you didn't tell tales. But if he didn't speak out, wouldn't he be guilty of letting Nathan get away with it?

And what about the people who had lost things? Farouk had lost an envelope with a £5 note in it to pay for a book he'd ordered. Didn't he owe it to Farouk and the other victims to say something?

Nathan and his mates were bullies. Jack was scared of them. If he said anything, they'd be sure to find out and he was terrified that they would beat him up.

Talk about the different courses of action that Jack could take. For example:

- Say nothing.
- Tell Miss Henshaw.
- Ask a friend for advice.
- Tell his parents.
- Confront Nathan.
- Leave an anonymous note for Miss Henshaw.
- Confide in an adult he trusts and ask their advice.

List them on the whiteboard and discuss what the consequences of each action might be. Ask: What would you do if you were Jack? Invite a few of them to share what they would do.

Conclusion
End with this prayer:

> Give us the courage to stand up for what is right.
> Let us choose the harder right instead of the easier wrong.
> Let us be prepared to stand firm when others try to force us to do what we know is wrong.
> Give us the strength not to give in however much pressure is put on us.
> Let what we know to be right always influence our behaviour, so that we treat others fairly and with consideration.

Thoughts for the day
> Wrong is wrong even if everyone is doing it. Right is right even if you are the only person doing it.
> > Unknown

23

Stand up for what you know is right, even if you stand alone.
Suzy Kassem

Further resources
A plan for an assembly on the theme of courage and sticking up for what you know to be right is available from the Assembly Box website.

RIGHTS AND RESPONSIBILITIES

Aim
To understand the rights that children have and the responsibilities that come with these rights.

Preparation
You could prepare one of these songs to sing before or after the class performance: 'If I Had a Hammer' by Pete Seeger and Lee Haye; 'I Won't Back Down' by Tom Petty.

Invite a class to prepare a presentation in which they show what rights children have and what responsibilities they have with regard to these rights. The class can be divided into two groups. One group is to decide what rights children have and produce banners for each of the rights. The other group focusses on the responsibilities that children have and produces banners stating what those responsibilities are.

This table shows what rights and responsibilities the groups should include:

Children's rights	Children's responsibilities
The right to a home	To keep it clean and nice
The right to have enough to eat	To eat a healthy diet
The right to keep warm	To avoid wasting energy

The right to be safe from physical and mental abuse	To tell an adult about what is happening
The right to be listened to	To tell the truth and to listen to others
The right to go to school	To make the most of the opportunities school offers
The right to have a religion	To allow others to practise their religion
The right to have friends	To treat your friends with respect
The right to express your opinions	To listen to the opinions of others

Introduction

Explain that the theme of the assembly is the rights you have as a human being and as a child. Talk about how everyone has certain rights – the right to a name, the right to belong to a family, the right to have a home. Explain that while we have these rights it is our responsibility to see that others have the rights too, and that having rights means we have responsibilities too.

Main focus: Children's rights and responsibilities

Invite the class to give the presentation which they have prepared.

Explain that throughout the world there are many children who are denied their rights. In countries where there is a war, children may be forced to leave school to become child soldiers. In other countries they may be denied an education because they come from marginalised communities. Their family may be so poor that they have to work all day instead of going to school. In India, for example, millions of children are denied an education because they have to work.

Conclusion

End with the thought for the day.

Thought for the day

Every child has the right to life, dignity, respect, leisure, liberty, health, education and shelter.

RULES

Aim
To understand why we have rules – at home, in school and in society.

Preparation
You could prepare these songs for the children to listen to as they enter and leave the hall: 'Breaking the Rules' by AC/DC; 'Rule the World' by Take That; 'New Rules' by Dua Lipa.

Choose a class to think about rules and why we have them. Some rules are written down; others, like the rules families have at home, are unwritten. Explain that you want the class to focus on rules at home and to prepare a presentation for an assembly about rules. Split the class into groups and give each group one of these 10 'Rules at home'.

Rules at home
- If you want someone to do something for you, say please.
- If someone does something for you, say thank you.
- If you make a promise, keep it.
- If it's your turn to do something, don't complain.
- If you make a mess, clear it up.
- If you break something, own up and try to fix it.
- If you want to borrow something, ask permission first.
- If you borrow something, make sure you return it.
- If you forget to do something, admit you forgot.
- If someone does or says something hurtful, be prepared to forgive them.

Ask each group to prepare to present a rule and say why families have that rule. Choose some members of the class to sum up what they learn from this activity about why families have rules, and to suggest other rules that families have, e.g. rules about swearing, table manners and respecting each other's views.

Introduction: The rules of the game
Start by asking the children to think of a game. Prompt them to think of different types of games such as sports, e.g. rugby, football,

tennis and netball; playground games, e.g. hopscotch; and board games, such as draughts, chess, 'Monopoly' and 'Deal or No Deal'. Ask: What do all these games have in common? Answer: They all have rules.

Ask: Why do the games have rules? Invite them to think of a rule. What would happen if the game did not have that rule? What would happen if the game had no rules?

Ask: What would happen if we didn't have rules in society? Who can think of an important rule that we have in our society? Explain that we have rules to protect ourselves from attack and our property from being damaged or stolen.

Main focus: Rules for family life

Invite the class to give the presentation they have prepared. Then put the rules for families up on the screen. Include the other rules that are suggested along with the 10 rules that the class focussed on.

Conclusion

End the assembly by asking which of the rules that apply to the family also apply when you are in school. Point out that they are all rules which we should follow in our behaviour towards other people, and so we should follow them in school as well as at home.

Thought for the day

Let us respect other members of our family. Let us be honest with each other and keep our promises. Let us share without complaining. Above all, let us treat others as we expect them to treat us.

Further resources

A PowerPoint presentation, 'Our Rules', is available from Primary Works. It emphasises what constitutes good manners in school and in class and the rules that children should follow.

SAYING SORRY

Aim
To explore the importance of acknowledging when you have done something wrong, and of apologising.

Preparation
Invite a class or a group of children to prepare to present the poems 'The Vase' and 'I Want to Say Sorry'.

Prepare the song 'Sorry Seems to Be the Hardest Word' by Blue ft. Elton John to play after the class presentation.

The Vase
> We've picked up all the pieces.
> We've brushed and swept the floor.
> We're waiting, listening for the click
> Of Mum's key in the door.
>
> We're wondering how to tell her.
> We're wondering how to say
> We broke the vase her Grandma gave her
> On her wedding day.

I Want to Say Sorry
> I want to say sorry
> But I don't know how
> I shouldn't have done it.
> I know that now.
>
> I didn't mean to do it.
> It was a stupid thing to do
> But I don't know how
> To apologise to you.
>
> I want to say sorry
> But I don't know how
> I shouldn't have done it.
> I know that now.

Introduction
Introduce the theme of the assembly by asking:

> Think of a time when you have had to apologise to your parents for something that you have done. For example, you may have forgotten to do something that they asked you to do, lost something or broken something of value. How difficult was it to say sorry?

Main focus: How to say sorry
Invite the class which has prepared the two poems to present them.

Put these statements up on the screen and ask some of the children to say whether or not they agree with them.

- 'It's best to own up and say sorry as soon as you've done something wrong.'
- 'It's easier to say sorry if you say it at once.'
- 'If you say sorry immediately, people will be more likely to accept your apology.'
- 'It's no good saying sorry unless you mean it.'

Conclusion
End by explaining that there are four things you should do when making an apology.

1. Be polite. Ask politely if you can speak to the person you have offended. For example, say: 'Excuse me. Can I talk to you about something?'
2. State clearly what you did. Admit what happened. Don't try to make excuses.
3. Be sincere. For example, admit that you made a mistake or shouldn't have done what you did.
4. Take responsibility. For example, say: 'I'm sorry. I shouldn't have behaved as I did.' Acknowledge your responsibility. Don't say things like 'I'm sorry if . . .' or 'I'm sorry you felt . . .'

Thought for the day
'Sorry' is just a word. It does not excuse you from having done things that you shouldn't do.

TOLERANCE

Aim
To understand that it is our responsibility to respect and tolerate people who are different from us.

Preparation
Download the songs 'Put Your Hands in the Air' and 'Acceptance Is the Word' from the website www.songspun.com.

Introduction
Explain that the theme of the assembly is tolerance. Ask: What does the word 'tolerance' mean?

Choose a number of children to give their answers, then give them a dictionary definition of 'tolerance': accepting and respecting differences between people.

Explain that the opposite of tolerance is intolerance: an unwillingness or refusal to respect people who are different or who hold opinions and beliefs different to one's own.

Main focus: The effects of intolerance
Tell the children that when you came to school this morning, there was a message waiting for you from the government containing details of certain children who were not to be allowed out at breaktime or dinner time and were to have an extra hour added on to their school day. This was due to their appearance, which the government was no longer prepared to tolerate. You were asked to identify the children in assembly.

Ask all the children to stand up, and explain that you are going to read the list to identify those whose appearance or behaviour is considered intolerable. If they are identified they are to sit down.

The list of children whose appearance or behaviour is considered intolerable is:

- Children with blue eyes.
- Children wearing a watch.
- Any child whose birthday is in January.
- Any child who is wearing a plaster.
- Any child who wears glasses.
- Any child with hair that is longer than shoulder length.
- Anyone who came to school on a bicycle.
- Any child who has a packed lunch.
- Anyone who had cereal for breakfast.

By the end of the list few, if any, children will be left standing.

Ask those left standing to sit down, and explain that this shows you what it would be like if groups of children were picked on and not tolerated for some reason.

Explain that in society groups are sometimes the victims of intolerance. For example, because of their race or religion. In history, there are many examples of such intolerance, e.g. of Jewish people.

Then read the poem 'Never Mind Your Creed or Colour' and discuss the message it contains about tolerating those who are different from ourselves.

Never Mind Your Creed or Colour
    Never mind your creed or colour
    You're my sisters and my brothers
    And together we will stand
    Hand in hand.

    Never mind our differences
    We won't build walls and fences
    And together we will stand
    Side by side.

    Never mind what clothes you wear
    How you cover up your hair
    We will walk the path together
    Step by step.

Never mind your creed or colour
We are sisters. We are brothers.
And respecting one another
We stand hand in hand.

Conclusion

Encourage everyone to join in and sing either 'Put Your Hands in the Air' or 'Acceptance Is the Word', which stress the importance of showing respect for those whose opinions, religion or race are different from our own.

Thoughts for the day

Tolerance means respecting other people's religious and cultural beliefs.

Tolerance means accepting that people have different opinions.

CHAPTER 2
Health and wellbeing

ANGER

Aim
To understand that it is important to think about times when you get angry and to learn to control your anger.

Preparation
Prepare to show two clips of children talking about how to manage anger from BBC Bitesize: 'How to cope with feeling angry' and 'Coping with feeling angry'.

You could prepare the Oasis song 'Don't Look Back in Anger' to include at the end of the assembly.

Make a large dial with the numbers 0–10 and fix an arrow on it to act as the Anger Indicator (see below).

Introduction
Explain that the theme of the assembly is anger and that you are going to begin by asking them to think about what makes them angry.

Main focus: What makes you angry?
Choose up to four children to take part in a survey of what makes them angry, and ask them to express the level of their anger on a scale of nought (if they are hardly angry at all) to 10 (when they are extremely angry). The children take it in turns to think about one of the situations listed below. When they have decided how angry it makes them, they move the arrow on the Anger Indicator to show the level of their anger. Invite comments from the audience, saying why they agree or disagree with their decision.

It makes me angry . . .

- When my parents won't let me go out.
- When someone bosses me about.
- When I'm very tired and hungry.
- When someone makes fun of my name.
- When they won't let me join their game.
- When someone barges in a queue.
- When I can't do what I wanted to.
- When I play a game and I lose.
- When I'm not allowed to choose.
- When I'm told off for something and didn't do it.
- When someone borrows something without asking.
- When my best friend does better than me in a test.
- When I am accused of something I didn't do.
- When the football team I support gets beaten.
- When I am made to do something I don't want to do.
- When I can't watch the programme I want to watch.
- When I have to stay in rather than go out with my friends.
- When I'm told off for being rude.
- When I see someone being bullied.
- When someone says something about me behind my back.
- When someone calls me a liar.
- When someone who hasn't seen me for a while says, 'Haven't you grown!'
- When the bus is late and I get told off for being late.

Main focus: Dealing with anger
Show the two clips of children talking about feeling angry and talking about how to manage their anger, available from BBC Bitesize.

Ask: What do you think is the best piece of advice that these children give? Write a list of their suggestions on the board. Talk about the importance of keeping calm and finding a way of managing your anger that works for you.

Put the words of 'If You're Angry and You Know It' on the board and encourage everyone to sing it to the tune of 'If You're Happy and You Know It'.

If You're Angry and You Know It
> If you're angry and you know it, remain calm.
> If you're angry and you know it, remain calm.
> If you're angry and you know it, keep your temper, do not lose it.
> If you're angry and you know it, remain calm.
>
> If you're angry and you know it, do not shout.
> If you're angry and you know it, do not shout.
> If you're angry and you know it, do not shout and scream and lose it.
> If you're angry and you know it, do not shout.
>
> If you're angry and you know it, don't lash out.
> If you're angry and you know it, don't lash out.
> If you're angry and you know it, just be careful how you show it.
> If you're angry and you know it, don't lash out.
>
> If you're angry and you know it, explain why.
> If you're angry and you know it, explain why.
> If you're angry and you know it, tell them why, then they will know it.
> If you're angry and you know it, tell them why.

Main focus: Righteous anger

Talk about how anger can be a positive reaction and explain that sometimes it is right to be angry. For example, how would you feel if you saw someone kicking a dog or hitting a baby?

What Makes You Angry, Mum?
> 'What makes you angry, Mum?' I asked.
> 'People who lie, and cheat and steal.
> But most of all, people who couldn't care less
> about what other people feel.'

Read the poem and talk about the things make Mum angry. Ask: Are there things that you think are wrong and you think it is right to be angry about?

Conclusion
End with one or more of the thoughts for the day.

Thoughts for the day
An old Cherokee told his grandson: 'My son, there is a battle between two wolves inside us all. One is Evil. It is anger, jealousy, greed, resentment, inferiority, lies and ego. The other is Good. It is joy, peace, love, hope, humility, kindness and truth.'

The boy thought about it and asked: 'Grandfather, which wolf wins?'

The old man quietly replied: 'The one you feed.'

> Holding on to anger is like grasping a hot coal with the intent of throwing it at someone else; you are the one that gets burned.
> Buddha

> If you are patient in one moment of anger, you will escape 100 days of sorrow.
> Chinese proverb

> Even though you disagree, do not refuse to listen.
> African proverb

What should you keep because no one else wants it? Your temper.

Further resources
A PowerPoint presentation on managing anger is available from Primary Works.

EATING HEALTHILY

Aim
To understand the importance of eating healthily.

Preparation
Make certificates to give to children who complete any of the challenges listed below.

Download the song-sheet 'Oh! What a Waste' from the Christian Aid website.

Prepare to play the 'Healthy Food vs Junk Food' song on YouTube.

Introduction

Remind the children of why we need to eat: so that we can get enough of the nutrients we need to keep our bodies fit and healthy.

Explain that this assembly is to launch Healthy Eating Week.

Main focus: Healthy foods and junk foods

Start with these jokes.

- What do refuse collectors eat? Junk food.
- Why did the schoolgirl eat her homework? Because the teacher told her it was a piece of cake.

Ask: What are healthy foods? Talk about why they are healthy.

Ask: What are junk foods? Why do we call them junk foods?

Play the video 'Healthy Food vs Junk Food' and invite the children to sing the song.

Food challenges

Explain that there are a number of challenges that the children could undertake as part of Healthy Eating Week. They could be either a daily challenge or a week-long challenge. Ask the children if anyone can suggest what the challenges night be, prompting them if necessary by giving them examples:

Examples of daily challenges	Examples of weekly challenges
'Drink wisely, drink plenty' day (i.e. lots of water, no fizzy drinks)	'No sweets' week
	'No savoury snacks' week (e.g. no crisps)
Try something new today	'No extra sugar' week
Make today a 'Five-a-day' day	'Fifteen minutes' exercise a day' week
'No chocolate' day	'No added salt' week

Encourage the children to take up one of the challenges. Hold up an example of the certificates they can get for completing one of the challenges. The classes can compete with each other to see which can complete the most challenges.

Further resources
Healthy Eating Week is organised annually by the British Nutrition Foundation. It produces a range of resources, including PowerPoint presentations such as 'The Amazing Lunchbox', which tells a story about a group of children and what they have in their lunchboxes.

Detailed ideas for an assembly on healthy living can be found at www.greatgrubclub.com.

An assembly on being 'sugar smart' is available at www.school wellbeing.co.uk.

EXERCISE

Aim
To explain why exercise is important.

Preparation
Ask a class to learn and prepare a presentation of 'The Exercise Rap'.

Introduction
Ask: How much exercise do you do each week? Put up your right hand if you think you take enough exercise, and your left hand if you think you should take more. Explain that the theme of the assembly is taking exercise.

Main focus: Why is exercise important?
Talk about what adults say about exercise. Ask: Why do they say it's good for you?

Put up the points that the children make so that you build up a list of reasons that you can put up in each classroom. The list should include the following:

- Exercise makes your heart beat faster and keeps it healthy.
- It helps your breathing and keeps your lungs healthy.
- It builds up your muscles and makes you stronger.
- It helps to control your weight by using up the energy you get from food, which otherwise is stored as fat.
- It keeps you fit and relaxed.

Ask the class which had prepared the presentation to perform 'The Exercise Rap'.

The Exercise Rap
> *(Chorus)*
> Put your hands together. Clap! Clap! Clap!
> Let's all do the exercise rap!
> There are all types of exercise you can do.
> What type you choose is up to you.
>
> You can jump. You can skip. You can run. You can hop.
> You can dance, dance, dance until you drop.
> You can play catch with a tennis ball.
> You can kick a football against a wall.
>
> *(Chorus)*
>
> You can walk or ride a bike to school.
> You can go for a swim in a swimming pool
> You can play a game of basketball.
> You can climb to the top of a climbing wall.
>
> *(Chorus)*
>
> You can take up gymnastics or judo.
> Fencing, karate or tai-kwon-do.
> You can run about a netball court.
> You can take up any kind of sport.
>
> *(Chorus)*
>
> Exercise will stop you from putting on weight.
> So don't put it off. Don't hesitate.
> Don't sit in front of the computer all day.
> Get off your backside. Go out and play.
>
> It doesn't matter what you choose to do.
> So long as you exercise it's up to you.

The exercise challenge

Explain that health experts consider that children should exercise for 60 minutes each day.

Challenge the children to keep a chart for the week, on which they record the exercise they do each day. You can download and print out a chart which the children can fill in from www.bbc. co.uk/northernireland/schools/4_11/uptoyou/healthy/food fitness.shtml.

Give out certificates at the end of the week to those who succeeded in doing 60 minutes of exercise each day.

Conclusion

End with the thoughts for the day.

Thoughts for the day

Make exercise part of your routine, like brushing your teeth or taking a shower. Don't think about doing it. Just do it!

Don't make excuses not to exercise such as 'I'm too tired,' 'It's too cold,' 'I haven't got the time' or 'I'll do it tomorrow.' It's about making time and doing it regularly every day.

HAPPINESS

Aim

To think about what happiness is and what makes us feel happy.

Preparation

Prepare for the assembly by asking the children in each class to write statements about happiness to put on a Happiness Chart. The statements could begin in several ways: 'Happiness is . . .', 'I felt happy when . . .', 'What makes me happy is . . .' or 'I would be very happy if . . .'

The classes can display their charts on the wall in their classrooms.

You could prepare a recording of 'Happy' by Pharrell Williams, which could be sung at the start of the assembly.

Introduction

Explain that March 20 is International Happiness Day.

Invite a representative from each class to read out some of the statements that their class made, as a way of introducing the theme of the assembly.

Ask whether some of the reasons for feeling happy are more important than others. For example, you may be happy when the football team that you support wins, or when you score a goal. Compare these feelings with feeling happy because someone you know has had a successful serious operation.

Main focus: What influences us to feel happy?

Read this poem:

Some Days
> Some days
> A stream of light
> Fills my mind.
> Everything's bright
> And the world
> Seems at ease,
> Bubbling with promise,
> As if someone
> Has thrown open the shutters
> Letting the sunlight pour in.
> And I feel happy.

Talk about how happy we feel can depend on lots of things, such as how well we feel, how tired we are, how hungry we are.

Talk about what you can do to make other people feel happy. For example, by greeting them with a smile, by telling a joke and making them laugh, by sharing something with them, by offering a helping hand.

Read them some jokes from a joke book or share some of these knock-knock jokes.

> Knock, Knock.
> Who's there?
> Howard.
> Howard who?
> Howard you know if you won't even open the door?

> Knock, knock.
> Who's there?
> Felix.
> Felix who?
> Felix my ice-cream, I'll lick his.

> Knock, knock.
> Who's there?
> Luke.
> Luke who?
> Luke through the letter-flap and see for yourself.

> Knock knock.
> Who's there?
> Rice Krispies.
> Rice Krispies who?
> I'll tell you next week. It's a cereal.

Encourage the children to write out their favourite jokes to put up during the day in their classrooms. Classes can vote for their favourite and include it on their class news page.

Thought for the day

> If you want to be happy for an hour – take a nap.
> If you want to be happy for a day – go fishing.

If you want to be happy for a year – inherit a fortune.
If you want to be happy for a lifetime – help someone else.

Chinese proverb

Conclusion
End the assembly with the song 'If You're Happy and You Know It'.

Further resources
Email info@actionforhappiness.org for resources which can be used to follow up the assembly. For example, there are activities such as interviewing a friend to find out about what things make them feel happy and making compliment cards to give to other children.

SADNESS

Aim
To explore feelings of sadness and how to cope with them.

Preparation
Make a large dial with the numbers 1–10 on it and a set of cards numbered 1–10.

Introduction: Feeling sad
Explain that sometimes we feel happy and sometimes we feel sad, and that the aim of the assembly is to explore what makes us feel sad, and to think about different levels of sadness and how to cope with sadness.

Main focus: Different levels of sadness
Explain that you are going to read out a number of statements and that you are going to carry out a survey to find out what things make people feel a little sad, quite sad and very sad. Choose six

people to act as a panel and give each of them a set of cards. Ask another teacher to hold the 'Sadometer' – the dial with the numbers 0–10 on it. After each statement each member of the panel has to decide where they would put it on the Sadometer – 1–3 is a little bit sad, 4–6 quite sad and 7–10 very sad. The teacher with the Sadometer works out the average score and moves the arrow to the appropriate point on the Sadometer.

Put these statements up on the board one by one and write the Sadometer scores next to them.

- Your friend tells you that she is moving to another school.
- The football match you were really looking forward to is cancelled.
- An elderly relative dies.
- A friend is seriously injured in a crash.
- A pet dog or cat is run over.
- You do not get the part you wanted in the school play.
- You have to move house and go to live in a different area.
- Your parents tell you that they are going to separate.
- You do badly in a test.

Talk about what the scores on the Sadometer reveal about levels of sadness and how the death of a relative makes us feel the saddest, and how sadness is part of grieving for someone.

Read what Erica Stewart says below about coping with sadness. Ask: Which piece of her advice do you think is the most helpful? Encourage the children to use a five-point scale by holding up the fingers of one hand to indicate how many stars they would give that piece of advice.

What can you do if you are feeling sad?

There are certain things you can do if you are feeling sad, says Erica Stewart. If you are feeling very sad, it can help to have a good cry. It's not babyish to cry and the idea that boys should not cry was abandoned long ago. Having a good cry lets your feelings out and it's better to cry than to bottle up your feelings.

Other things you can do are take some exercise, like going for a cycle ride or going for a swim. Taking exercise can take your mind off what's making you sad.

Or do an activity that you enjoy. You can play your favourite computer game or watch your favourite film. Listening to your favourite music can help too.

And if your friends call round for you, try to make yourself go out with them, even though you don't feel like it.

Don't spend all your time moping and feeling sorry for yourself; it won't help. What will help is if you talk to someone about your feelings. If you feel you can't talk to Mum or Dad about it, find an adult you can trust.

Stress that it is important to recognise what makes us feel sad and to learn to cope with our feelings of sadness.

Conclusion
End with the thought for the day.

Thought for the day
You cannot prevent the birds of sadness passing over your head, but you can prevent them from making a nest in your hair.

Chinese proverb

SAFER INTERNET DAY

Aim
To explain how to keep safe on the internet.

Preparation
Download the PowerPoint on e-safety from the Primary Resources website: www.primaryresources.co.uk/ict/ict3.htm.

Visit the Safer Internet Day (SID) site to find out about how you can obtain their education pack. There are separate films for infants and juniors available on YouTube. A good way of capturing the interest of infants is to include the SID film 'Ask Before You Watch' aimed at 5- to 7-year-olds.

Ask one of the classes to prepare a reading of the poem 'Surf the Net Safely'. Encourage the class to make posters which they can hold up while presenting the poem. After the assembly, put the posters up around the school.

Introduction
Explain that today is Safer Internet Day. Begin with a joke:

- What goes 'choo choo choo' when it is online? Thomas the search engine.

Then talk about how important it is to stay safe when they are using the internet.

Main focus: Staying safe on the internet
Either begin by showing the SID film 'Ask Before You Watch' or by reading Stephen's story below. If you use the story, talk about what he did. Ask the children:

- Is it OK to go on the internet to chat to other children?
- How can you tell if a chat site is safe?
- Do you always ask an adult to check what sites you are visiting?
- How can you tell if somebody is who they say they are?
- Have any of the children had an experience like Stephen's that they are willing to share?
- How did they deal with it?
- What should Stephen do?

Scenario: Stephen's story
>   We live on a farm. The nearest house is in a village about four miles away, so I don't have any friends living nearby. I go on the internet and enjoy chatting to people. I've made several friends from different parts of the country. There was one particular

friend who said he was called Bill. He said he was my age and that he lived only 10 miles away. He wanted to meet up, so I agreed. He said not to tell anyone. It would be more fun if we met in secret. I didn't tell my parents, but I told my older brother. He said he'd come along with me to make sure everything was alright. What a good job he did! Bill turned out to be a man of 40. He hurried off when he saw I wasn't alone.

Present the PowerPoint on e-safety.

End the assembly with the class presenting the poem 'Surf the Net Safely', then everyone singing the song 'Stay Safe on the Internet', which can be found on the Assembly Tube website.

Surf the Net Safely
Surf the net safely.
When online don't share
Your personal details.
Take care. Be aware.

There are adults out there
Who will pretend
To be young like you
And to be your friend.

Don't be fooled into thinking
They aren't a stranger.
Remember the risks.
You may be in danger.

If you get an email
And don't recognise
Who sent it to you
Be wary. Be wise.

Before you make a download
Just stop and think.
Could there be a virus
If you click on the link?

Surf the net safely.
And be well aware
When using the internet
Always take care.

Conclusion
End with the thought for the day, emphasising how important the message it gives is.

Thought for the day
Take care when you share. If in doubt, speak out.

The NSPCC

Further resources
A set of online internet safety posters which you can put up around the school is available from www.free-for-kids.com.

The Share Aware resources produced by the NSPCC have two lesson plans, which can be used following the assembly with Key Stage 2 classes, dealing with chatting safely online and the risks involved if you post pictures online.

A number of sites have internet safety quizzes which can be used to reinforce the messages conveyed in the assembly, such as those which can be found on the Safekids and QuizMoz websites.

SAFETY AT HOME

Aim
To increase children's awareness of the causes of accidents at home and of how to stay safe in their homes.

Preparation
Put up a picture of a living room showing a number of hazards. For example, you could use the picture of the living room shown on the Nationwide Education website: www.nationwideeducation.co.uk/collection/being-safe-at-home. Find a similar picture of dangers in the kitchen.

Introduction
Explain that more accidents occur at home than anywhere else.

- The most common types of accidents in the home are falls.
- Boys are more likely to have accidents than girls.
- Two million children each year attend A&E departments following accidents at home.
- Over 4,000 children a year are injured in falls on stairs.
- The most common place for accidents is the lounge/living room.

Main focus: Living room hazards and kitchen dangers
Put up the picture of the living room and ask the children how many dangers they can spot in the picture. Allow time for them to pick out the hazards, then ask individuals to name a danger and to explain why it is a danger. Make a list of the dangers on a flipchart, which can be typed up after the assembly and put up in each classroom.

Then put up a picture showing dangers in the kitchen and repeat the activity, asking the children to spot the dangers in the kitchen.

Conclusion
Present the safety slogans in 'Thought for the day' and challenge the children to think up safety slogans of their own. They can put the slogans up around the school and you can run a competition with prizes for the winning slogans.

Thoughts for the day
Safety starts with an S, but begins with YOU.

Safety is as simple as ABC – Always Be Careful.

Further resources
Interactive activities for infants and lower juniors can be found at www.nationwideeducation.co.uk.

SAFETY IN THE STREET AND OUTDOORS

Aim
To explain how to stay safe in the street and when playing outside.

Preparation
Download the PowerPoint 'Keeping Safe Outside School' from the Primary Resources website.

Prepare to play the video of the song 'Three Ways to Stay Safe' on YouTube.

Introduction
Tell them Jenny's story.

Scenario: Jenny's story

One day Jenny was walking home from school alone, as she had had to stay behind after school for a play rehearsal. Normally she walked home with Prisa, but today Prisa was ill. As she approached the turning off the High Street, which would take her down the lane towards her home, she became aware of someone behind her.

She looked over her shoulder and saw a young man wearing dark glasses. Her instinct told her that there was something sinister about him and she felt threatened by him. She quickened her pace and as she did so, he too quickened his pace.

Jenny decided to walk past the entrance to the lane and stay on the High Street. When she did so, she sensed the man was drawing level with her. She saw a woman coming in the opposite direction, so she yelled 'Help!' At once the man turned and ran off. The woman asked her what the matter was.

Jenny started to cry. 'I was frightened,' she said. 'Someone was following me.' The woman gave Jenny a tissue. 'You did the right thing, pet,' the woman said.

Ask: Did Jenny do the right thing? Then ask: What safety tips can you suggest for walking to and from school? List their suggestions on the board. Here is an example of such a list.

Be 'street smart':

- Do not walk alone. Stick with a friend.
- Ignore any stranger who tries to speak to you.
- Don't trust a stranger even if he says he knows your mum.
- Stay near safe spots, e.g. stay on busy streets even if it takes longer.
- Avoid places that are unsafe such as narrow unlit streets or lonely lanes.
- Always trust your instincts. If you feel threatened, get away from the area and tell your parents or the police.

Main focus: Keeping yourself safe in the street and when playing outside

Use the PowerPoint 'Keeping Safe Outside School'. Discuss the slides one by one. Ask: What safety message does that particular slide give?

Ask: What are places where you shouldn't play and things you should never do when playing outside?

Make a list and put it up on the screen. Your list could include:

- Never ignore 'Danger' signs.
- Never jump or dive into a lake or river.
- Never go on a frozen pond or lake unless the ice is very thick.
- Never play with farm machinery.
- Never fly a kite near electricity pylons.
- Never play on a building site.
- Never play near railway lines.
- Stay away from slippery banks of rivers and canals.
- Do not play in caves or quarries.
- Do not play hide-and-seek in a forest.
- Do not play beside a motorway or dual carriageway.

Conclusion

End by playing the song 'Three Ways to Stay Safe'.

Thoughts for the day
To avoid the worst, put safety first.

Be safe, not sorry.

Further resources
The Water Safety Code providing advice on why it is dangerous to swim in lakes or rivers can be found at the Royal Society for the Prevention of Accidents (ROSPA) website.

SAFETY ON THE ROAD

Aim
To teach the children how to cycle safely.

Preparation
Invite a class to do a presentation of 'The Safe Cycling Rap'.

Prepare sets of red and green cards for the children to hold up (see 'Main focus' below).

The Safe Cycling Rap
> Don't be a fool. Just play it cool.
> Follow these cycling safety rules.
>
> When you ride, without exception
> Wear a helmet for protection.
>
> Check your brakes before your ride.
> Have the tyres got enough air inside?
>
> Keep your hands on the handlebars.
> Don't ride into the road between parked cars.
>
> Don't you ride on the pavement, man,
> Unless a sign says that you can.

Don't wear headphones. You won't hear a shout
Or a horn that warns you to look out.

Never ride at night without a light.
Wear a high-vis jacket that's yellow and bright.

Always ride at the side of the road
And make sure you follow the Highway Code.

Don't be a fool. Just play it cool.
Cycle safely – just follow these rules.

Introduction
Explain that the theme of the assembly is to understand how to ride
your bicycle safety.

Main focus: Rules to follow when riding your bicycle
Read Lester's story.

Lester's story
> Lester had overslept. It was games day. So as he went out
> of the door he grabbed his PE kit. He slung it over the han-
> dlebars of his bike. He'd forgotten his helmet, but he was
> already very late. He shot across the pavement, straight onto
> the road in front of an oncoming car. He tried to swerve, but
> lost control as his PE bag got caught in the front wheel. He
> was thrown into the air and landed awkwardly. He had to go
> to A&E. He had a broken arm, but as the nurse said, he was
> lucky he didn't land on his head.

Ask: What do you learn about cycling safely from Lester's story?
Points to make are:

- Never put anything on the handlebars of your bicycle.
- Always wear a helmet.
- Don't ride straight across the pavement onto the road.

True or false?

Make sure that each child has a red card and a green card.

Explain that you are going to read out a number of statements and they have to decide whether the statement is true or false and hold up a green card for 'true' and a red card for 'false'.

- Boys are more likely to be injured in bicycle accidents than girls. *(True – 80% of those injured in cycling accidents are males.)*
- More accidents occur in daylight than in the dark. *(True – the most dangerous times for cyclists are 3.00 pm to 6 pm and 8 am to 9 am.)*
- Children under 10 are more likely to be involved in cycling accidents than teenagers. *(False – 10- to 15-year-olds are more at risk than other age groups.)*
- You do not need to have lights on your bicycle when riding at night in an area with street lighting. *(False – it is an offence to ride on the road without lights when it is dark.)*
- A cyclist can be fined for jumping a red light. *(True – you can also be fined for riding on the pavement.)*
- It is against the law to give someone a lift on your bicycle. *(True – it is illegal because it is dangerous.)*
- Two-thirds of serious injuries in cycling accidents occur at road junctions. *(True – roundabouts are particularly dangerous, and cyclists need to take great care when turning right.)*
- Schools can stop you from riding your bicycle if you don't wear a helmet. *(False – a school can only insist on you wearing a helmet on the school premises. It cannot stop you riding on the road without a helmet.)*

Invite the class that has prepared it to perform 'The Safe Cycling Rap'.

Conclusion

Sum up by reminding the children: 'It's better to be safe than sorry and that it is dangerous to take chances when riding your bike.' Then introduce the three thoughts for the day.

Thoughts for the day
Accidents hurt. Safety doesn't.

Chance takers. Accident makers.

Know safety. No injury. No safety. Know injury.

Further resources
The ROSPA website has ideas for assemblies for 4- to 7-year-olds and 7- to 11-year-olds on crossing the road safely and cycling safely.

Encourage the children to play the cycling safety games which can be found at http://talesoftheroad.direct.gov.uk/cycling-safely.php.

CHAPTER 3
Global issues

ENDANGERED SPECIES

Aim
To understand what conservation means, which animals are in danger of extinction and why it is important to save them.

Preparation
Make three cards: one with *Endangered* on it, one with *Extinct* and one with *Not in danger*. Ask some children to draw pictures of the animals in the list (below) and to print the name of the animal underneath the picture.

Introduction
Explain that the theme of the assembly is conservation, and ask what conservation means – looking after the environment so that the animals and plants which live there can continue to do so.

Prepare to play 'The Animal Extinction Song' by the BBC and YouTubers, which can be used at the start or end of the assembly.

Endangered species
Because in the past mankind has not taken enough care of the environment, some species have died out and become extinct. Many others are endangered.

Ask three children to stand at the front holding the three cards *Endangered*, *Extinct* and *Not in danger* and the 12 children who drew the pictures to stand in a line at the front.

Ask: Do you know which animals have become extinct? Which are endangered? Explain that you are going to read out a list of animals (below) and ask the children to use their hands to indicate whether they think that species is safe at present (they should put their thumbs up), endangered (use their index fingers to indicate a warning) or extinct (put their thumbs down). When you read out the answer, the child with the picture of the animal goes and stands behind the child holding the card which says either *Endangered*, *Extinct* or *Not in danger*.

The animals are:

- Mammoth (extinct)
- Orang-utan (endangered)
- Crocodile (not in danger)
- Chimpanzee (endangered)
- Dodo (extinct)
- Blue whale (endangered)
- Grey wolf (not in danger)
- Shark (not in danger)
- Sabre-tooth tiger (extinct)
- Black rhino (extinct)
- Brown bear (not in danger)
- Snow leopard (endangered)

Ask: Why do some animals become extinct? Guide their answers to include:

- Climate change
- Destruction of habitats due to man-made activities, e.g. farming, logging, mining
- Hunting and poachers

Put 'If You Go Down to the Woods Today' on the board and invite the children to sing it to the tune of 'The Teddy Bears' Picnic'.

If You Go Down to the Woods Today
> If you go down to the woods today,
> you're in for a big surprise
> For they're chopping all the trees down
> To build a new high rise.

So all the animals that once lived there
Cannot live there today
Because today's the day
They are going to chop the trees down.

Homeless time for the animals
There's nothing that the animals can do
But watch in despair
Till the wood's no longer there
Because today's the day they chopped the trees down.

Conclusion
End by reading 'The Elephants' Prayer'.

The Elephants' Prayer
We are the mighty elephants.
We roam the land
In search of food and water.
Protect us, please,
From the wicked poachers with their guns,
Who shoot us for our ivory tusks,
Not caring about whether or not
We are in danger of being hunted
To extinction.
We are the mighty elephants.
Please protect us.

WORLD CONSERVATION DAY

Aim
To understand that the world's resources are not limitless and that we need to take steps to conserve them.

Preparation
Prepare to show a video clip from the World Wildlife Fund, 'Saving Wildlife' (available from iSpot.tv), which stresses how we need to conserve the world's resources.

You could prepare a recording of these two songs for the children to sing at an appropriate point in the assembly: 'Radioactive' by Imagine Dragons and 'It's the End of the World as We Know It' by REM.

Introduction
Explain that December 4 is World Conservation Day and talk about the meanings of the words 'conservation' and 'sustainability'.

Talk about how the world's resources are not inexhaustible and if we don't look after them, at some point in the not-too-distant future they will run out.

Main focus: How humans are responsible for damaging the Earth
Put 'All Things Dry and Dusty' on the screen. Ask: What is the message of the poem? Discuss how different it is from the well-known song 'All Things Bright and Beautiful'. The children can then sing it to the tune of 'All Things Bright and Beautiful'.

All Things Dry and Dusty
>All things dry and dusty,
>All plants shrivelled and small,
>All trees bare and blighted,
>It's man who made them all.
>
>The shoots that twist and wither.
>The rotten leaves that fall,
>The fruits that do not ripen,
>It's man who made them all.
>
>All things dry and dusty,
>All plants shrivelled and small,
>All trees bare and blighted,
>It's man who made them all.
>
>The fields that yield no harvest,
>The empty market stall,

The orchard's fruitless trees,
It's man who made them all.

All things dry and dusty,
All plants shrivelled and small,
All trees bare and blighted,
It's man who made them all.

Main focus: What can we do to look after the world's resources?

Read the poem 'The Cliff's Edge' and talk about why it is called 'The Cliff's Edge'.

The Cliff's Edge
Step back! Step back!
Before it's too late.
The cliff edge is crumbling
It won't bear the weight

Of the things that we make
That we don't really need,
Of all of our selfishness,
All of our greed.

Stop now! Stop now!
Stop the fracking and drilling.
Stop the mining and digging.
It's the future we're killing

By spoiling the land
And poisoning the air
With gases that
Destroy the ozone layer.

Step back! Step back!
Don't hesitate.
The cliff edge is crumbling.
It'll soon be too late.

Ask the children to suggest what we can do to conserve resources.

What could governments do to stop us from falling over the cliff's edge? Talk about practical policies such as investing in renewable energy and encouraging people to use resource-friendly cars by taxing 'gas guzzlers'. Ask: What can individuals do? For example, turn the central heating down, once a room is warm enough; switch off lights when you leave a room; take a shower instead of a bath.

On a large sheet of paper make a chart with a line down the middle and stick Post-its on one side saying things that the government can do to conserve resources, and on the other side stating things which individuals can do.

Conclusion
Read the poem 'Keep Hope Alive'.

Keep Hope Alive
    Keep hope alive whatever you do
    For the Earth's future depends upon you.

    The fish in the sea, the birds in the air,
    The creatures on land all need our care.

    Don't take more than you need, just what is fair.
    Make sure that everyone has their fair share.

    Hope that the hungry will get what they need
    Don't let others starve because of your greed.

    Pray for peace and an end to all wars.
    Keep hope alive, for the future is yours.

    Remember the future depends on you
    And keep hope alive whatever you do.

Reinforce the message that we must act now before it is too late, by playing the video clip 'Saving Wildlife'.

Thought for the day
Explain that these thoughts are from the sayings of Native Americans:

Take only what you need and leave the land as you found it.

The frog does not drink up the pond in which he lives.

>May the Warm Winds of Heaven
>blow softly upon your house.
>May the Great Spirit
>bless all who enter there.
>May your moccasins
>make happy tracks in many snows
>and may the Rainbow
>always touch your shoulder.

Enjoy the Earth Gently
>Enjoy the Earth gently
>For if the Earth is spoiled
>It cannot be repaired.
>Enjoy the Earth gently.

Traditional African poem

WORLD FOREST DAY

This assembly can be used around March 21, which is World Forest Day.

Aim
To understand why the world's forests are disappearing and why it is important to preserve them.

Preparation
You can invite a year 5 or year 6 class to prepare an assembly consisting of a PowerPoint presentation about why the world's forests are disappearing and what the consequences of their destruction are.

They could also include a performance of the poem 'Where Is the Forest?' together with performances of any poems they find about trees and forests, such as Spike Milligan's 'Tree-Kill' from *Green Poems* (OUP), Richard Edward's 'Ten Tall Oak Trees' and David Harmer's 'Our Tree' from *Earthways, Earthwise* (OUP). They can include any poems they have written themselves; e.g. poems in the form of prayers in which the animals ask for help to save their forest home.

Introduction
Introduce the topic by explaining that March 21 is World Forest Day. Ask: Why are forests important? Encourage them to look around the hall. What can they see that is made of wood? Make a list of the things they say; e.g. furniture and flooring, musical instruments, books and paper.

Ask: What else have humans used wood for? Making tools, building shelters and houses and fuel.

Explain that the consequence of humans using wood for so many different purposes has been the destruction of the world's forests.

Main focus: Why the destruction of the forests matters
Ask: Does it matter that the world's forests are being destroyed? Invite them to put up their hands if they think it does. Why do they think it matters? Point out that the world's forests are important because they support so many species of plants, insects and animals. They are also important because they absorb the greenhouse gases which cause climate change, and they protect the air we breathe by reducing the amount of carbon dioxide in the atmosphere.

Invite the class to give their PowerPoint presentation and read the poem 'Where Is the Forest?' Then identify the reasons the poem gives for why the forests are disappearing and ask the children to suggest what we as individuals can do to help preserve them for the future.

Note: A PowerPoint presentation of the poem is available from Primary Works.

Where Is the Forest?
Where is the forest?
cried the animals.
Where are the trees?

We needed the wood,
said the people.
Wood to make fires.
Wood for our houses.
We cut it down.

Where is the forest?
cried the animals.
Where are the trees?

We needed the land,
said the people.
Land for our cattle.
Land for our roads.
We cut it down.

Where is the forest?
cried the animals.
Where is our home?

Gone, whispered the wind.
Gone. Gone. Gone.

Conclusion
End with the thoughts for the day.

Thoughts for the day
It takes many years to grow a tree, but a day to cut it down.
African proverb

A nation that destroys its soils destroys itself. Forests are the lungs of our land, purifying the air and giving fresh strength to our people.

Franklin D. Roosevelt

WORLD HOMELESS DAY

Aim
To increase understanding of homelessness and its effects.

Preparation
Prepare a group of children from year 5 or 6 to participate by investigating the causes of homelessness and what it is like to have no home and to have to sleep rough or to live as a family in one room or in a tent. Invite them to prepare statements to read from individuals (see below).

Introduction
Explain that October 10 is World Homeless Day.

Begin by reading the poem 'Sitting in the Doorway'.

Sitting in the Doorway
Sitting in the doorway
With nothing to eat,
Feeling the cold
Biting my feet.
Sitting in the doorway
With nothing to do,
At the back of the line –
The end of the queue.

Sitting in the doorway
With nowhere to hide
From the night's bitter chill
And the hunger inside.

Sitting in the doorway
With nothing.

Ask one or two of the children to say what they pictured as you read the poem.

Explain that the poem can be interpreted as being about either a boy or a girl, a young man or young woman or an older person. It could be in a town in the UK or in a war zone, such as Syria.

Invite a group of children who have investigated why become homeless to present prepared statements about why they are homeless. The group should role-play people such as a teenager who left home because of family problems; or a young boy or girl who has become a refugee because of famine, or because their home was destroyed in a war, or because of religious persecution.

Talk about what it is like to have no home. Invite the group to role-play what it is like having no money and having to sleep rough, or for a homeless family having to live in one room or in a hostel.

Explain that charities in the UK, such as Shelter and St Mungo's, try to help people who are sleeping rough to put their lives back together.

Then read and discuss the poem 'My House'.

My House
> My house is not my house
> if there is someone without a house
> alongside my house.
>
> The thing is that my house
> can't be my house
> if it's not also the house
> of whoever has no house.

Anon

Conclusion
End with a prayer.

> Loving God, in your house there is room for everyone.
> Help us as we strive for a world where everyone has a home
> that truly meets their needs.

Give us the grace to welcome strangers and refugees.
Give us the insight to see where inequality hurts.
Fill us with the courage to do our part.
Save us from being overwhelmed by the scale of the housing crisis and show us, O Lord, where to begin. Amen.

Further resources

A useful website is www.congregational.org.uk/downloads/blogs/homeless-sunday.pdf.

WORLD HUNGER DAY

Aim

To increase awareness of the unfair distribution of food in the world and of the fact that a large number of people suffer from hunger and malnutrition.

Preparation

Download the video of 'Oh! What a Waste' from the Christian Aid website.

Songs to sing and listen to: 'Food Glorious Food' from the musical *Oliver* and 'Do They Know it's Christmas' by Band Aid.

Introduction

Talk about how much food gets thrown away at Christmas time. Play them a video of the song 'Oh! What a Waste' and invite them to sing along with it.

Main focus: The reasons why some people are hungry

Explain that in the world it is estimated that one in nine people do not get enough food to lead a healthy life. Ask: Why do you think this is?

Use their responses to make these points:

1. Poverty. People are too poor to be able to buy what they need.
2. Famines. People cannot grow what they need because the land has become desert, causing famines.
3. We grow enough food to feed everyone in the world but it is unfairly distributed.

Explain that in the European Union there are stores of grain and butter – food mountains – that could be used to help feed people in poorer countries.

Why are they hungry? A 'true or false' quiz
Explain that in African countries such as Somalia as many as half the population do not have enough to eat. Read these statements in turn and ask the children to put up one of their hands if they think the statement is true.

- African farmers are lazy. *(False.)*
- African farmers do not have enough good land on which to grow crops. *(True.)*
- There is not enough food in the world to feed everyone. *(False.)*
- African families have too many children. *(False.)*
- Some people in the world have more than their fair share. *(True.)*
- African farmers do not get paid a fair price for their produce. *(True.)*

Food banks
Talk about food banks. Ask: What is a food bank?

Explain that everyone should be able to have enough food to feed their families. But sometimes people do not have enough money to buy food. Even in rich countries like the UK there are families who cannot buy the food they need. So in England there are over 400 food banks. People donate foods in supermarkets. Charities then sort the foods and make up food parcels to distribute to those who cannot afford to buy it themselves.

Conclusion
End with a prayer.

> Let us think about how we can help those in the world who do not get enough to eat.
> Let us open our stores of grain and distribute it to those who are in need.
> Let us learn to share the food that we have, so that no one goes hungry.

Thought for the day

> Food is the moral right of all who are born into this world.
> Norman Borlaug

> If we can conquer space, we can conquer childhood hunger.
> Buzz Aldrin

> The world produces enough food to feed the entire population. It is a travesty that anyone should go hungry anywhere.
> Donny Osmond

Further resources
Further facts about this topic can be found at the World Hunger Day website.

WORLD OCEANS DAY

Aim
To understand what pollution is doing to the oceans and why it is important to take action to reduce it.

Preparation
Invite a class to prepare a PowerPoint presentation including information explaining why it is important to look after the oceans (see below) and giving facts about pollution of the ocean, such as:

- The biggest problem is caused by plastic, which does not degrade.
- Every year 8 million tons of plastic waste finds its way into the ocean.
- It is estimated that by 2050 there will be more plastic than fish in the ocean.
- Fish are being poisoned by eating microplastics – tiny pieces of plastic which they mistake for food.
- There are now half as many fish in the ocean as there were 50 years ago.
- Large areas of the ocean have become so full of plastic that they are known as 'great garbage patches'. There is one in the North Pacific Ocean and one in the South Pacific.

Encourage the class to make posters on which they state the reasons why we need to be concerned about polluting the oceans.

Prepare to show the video 'Keep the Oceans Clean' on YouTube.

Introduction
Explain that June 8 is World Oceans Day. Explain that we need to treat the oceans with care, but that the oceans are in danger because we have polluted them.

Main focus
Ask the class to present the PowerPoint. Then ask them to show the posters saying why it is important to look after the oceans.

Emphasise the points they have made, which should include:

- Oceans create most of the oxygen we breathe.
- They are an important source of food, providing protein for millions of people.
- They regulate our climate and weather.
- They are important for world trade – 90% of the goods we trade is transported on them.
- They can be used to provide renewable energy through wave power and wind farms.

Read the poem 'Then and Now'. Discuss what it says about how pollution is harming the oceans.

Then and Now
>Once only seaweed floated on the surface of the oceans
>Now there are great garbage patches of plastic.
>
>Once the fish that we caught and ate were free of toxins
>Now who knows what chemicals they have ingested?
>
>Once the sea was clean and the coral reefs flourished
>Now debris snags on the coral and the reefs are shrinking.
>
>Once only shells and stones were washed in by the waves
>Now our beaches are littered with rubbish the tide brings in.
>
>Once a multitude of seabirds filled the ocean's skies
>Now each year pollution kills a million seabirds.
>
>Once dolphins and porpoises swam freely
>Now they become entangled in trawlermen's nets.
>
>Once the ocean was clean and the fish and mammals were safe
>Now it is full of waste and all marine life is threatened.

Conclusion
Play the video of the song 'Keep the Oceans Clean' and invite the children to join in.

Thought for the day
>People ask: why should I care about the ocean? Because the ocean is the cornerstone of earth's life support system, it shapes climate and weather. It holds most of life on earth, 97% of earth's water is there. It is the blue heart of the planet – we should take care of our heart. It's what makes life possible.

We have a really good chance to make things better than they are. They won't get better unless we take the action and inspire others to do the same thing. No one is without power. Everyone has the capacity to do something.

Sylvia Earle, marine biologist

Further resources
Useful websites include www.worldoceansday.com.

WORLD PEACE DAY

World Peace Day is September 21.

Aim
To increase awareness of the consequences of war, and the need to try to resolve conflicts peacefully.

Preparation
If there are children in the school from refugee families who have fled to the UK because of war in their homeland, you can invite them or their parents to take part in the assembly. They can either give a short talk which can be incorporated into the assembly or you can interview them about their experiences.

Introduction
Ask the children: Where in the world are there wars going on? Do you know why these wars started? Guide the discussion so that the following points are made: Many wars are disputes over land. Others occur between people of different religions or different races or because people want to force a change of government.

Main focus: A world of peace
Ask: What is a pacifist? Explain that a pacifist is someone who will not fight in any circumstance. People who refused to fight in the two world wars were called 'conscientious objectors'. They were

called cowards by some people but many of them stuck to their principles and went to jail for their beliefs. Discuss the view that it takes more courage to be a pacifist than to fight.

Read the poem 'I Dream of a Time'.

I Dream of a Time

> I dream of a time
> when there's no more war
> when it's safe to walk the streets once more.
>
> I dream of a time
> when no bombs rain from the sky
> when no innocent civilians die.
>
> I dream of a time
> when soldiers from different lands
> put down their weapons and all shake hands.
>
> I dream of a time
> when conflicts between nations
> are settled by negotiations.
>
> I dream of a time
> when minefields are cleared,
> when you can walk paths that you once feared.
>
> I dream of a time
> when no one's forced to flee
> to become a stateless refugee.
>
> I hope for a time
> when the shooting stops and no one
> feels the need to carry a gun.
>
> I hope for a time when there's peace.

Discuss what the person in the poem says. How would the world have to change if his dream were to come true?

Conclusion

Sing the World Peace Day song 'No Wars Will Stop Us Singing' by Debbie Wiseman. The lyrics are available on YouTube.

End with 'The Eastener's Prayer'.

The Eastener's Prayer
> I pray the prayer that the Easteners do
> May the peace of Allah abide with you.
> Wherever you stay wherever you go
> May the beautiful palms of Allah grow;
> Through days of labour and nights of rest,
> The love of good Allah make you blest,
> So I touch my heart as Easteners do –
> May the peace of Allah abide with you!

Thoughts for the day

> It is no longer good enough to cry peace. We must act peace, live peace and live in peace.
>
> Native American proverb

> War is a bad chisel with which to carve out the future.
>
> African proverb

> Let us eat out of the same spoon and drink out of the same cup.
>
> African proverb

Further resources

A World Peace Day PowerPoint, available from TES Resources, includes a story, 'A Peacekids Adventure', by Steve Diamond and Robert Alan; a short video clip of Muhammad Ali with children around the world asking for peace; and a video promoting peace.

A pack of ideas for lessons and assemblies, 'Teach Peace', is available from the Peace Education Network.

WORLD RECYCLING DAY

Aim
To increase awareness of the importance of recycling.

Preparation
Choose a class to prepare an assembly on recycling. Encourage them to use the internet to find out about recycling and what they can do to reduce waste by recycling. Ask them to make a list, '10 Facts You Should Know about Recycling', or give them copies of the list below.

Encourage groups to think of ways of presenting the facts about recycling; e.g. by producing a scene in which Rita the Recycler and Ronald the Reuser catch two people called Willie Wasteful and Charlotte Couldn't-Careless throwing away items that could be recycled or reused and try to convince them of the importance of recycling and reusing. Invite one or two of the groups to perform their scenes as part of the assembly.

Ask the children in the class to write letters to their local newspaper drawing attention to the fact that it is World Recycling Day. Get one or two of them to read out the letters.

Encourage the class to learn and to present 'The Recycling Rap'.

The Recycling Rap
Listen to me, children. Hear what I say.
We've got to start recycling. It's the only way
To save this planet for future generations –
The name of the game is reclamation.
You've got to start recycling. You know it makes sense.
You've got to start recycling. Stop sitting on the fence.
No more pussyfooting. No more claptrap.
Get yourself doing the recycling rap.

Come on and start recycling. Start today
By saving old newspapers, not throwing them away.

Don't just take them and dump them on the tip;
Tie them in a bundle and put them in the skip.

Get collecting, protecting the future's up to you.
Save all your old glass bottles and your jam jars too.
Take them to the bottle bank, then at the factory
The glass can be recycled, saving energy.
Don't chuck away that empty drink can.
Remember what I said. Start recycling, man.
Wash it, squash it, squeeze it flat and thin.
Take it to the Save-A-Can and post it in.

Listen to me, children. Hear what I say.
We've got to start recycling. It's the only way
To save this planet for future generations –
The name of the game is reclamation.
You've got to start recycling. You know it makes sense.
You've got to start recycling. Stop sitting on the fence.
No more pussyfooting. No more claptrap.
Get yourself doing the recycling rap.

Introduction
Explain that the theme of assembly is recycling and that World Recycling Day is held in November.

Ask: What do we mean by recycling? Then ask: Why is recycling important?

Main focus: How much do you know about recycling?
Put up these statements one by one and ask them to put their thumbs up if they think the statement is true and their thumbs down if they think it is false.

- A plastic shopping bag can take over 100 years to decompose. *(True.)*
- Glass can be recycled again and again. *(True.)*
- The UK leads the world recycling more of its waste than other countries. *(False – countries such as Switzerland, Germany and the Netherlands recycle more than the UK.)*

- An average family throws away £100 worth of edible food every year. *(False – it is estimated that £470 is thrown away each year.)*
- Recycling is a waste of time because most of our waste ends up in landfill or is sent abroad. *(False.)*
- All kinds of plastic can be recycled. *(False.)*
- Burning rubbish in incinerators is better than putting it in the ground as landfill. *(True – incinerators cause less pollution than landfill sites, which produce methane.)*

Invite the class that has focussed on recycling to perform their presentation.

Put the following version of 'Ten Green Bottles' on the screen and get the children to join in singing it to the tune of 'Ten Green Bottles':

Ten Green Bottles
> Ten green bottles.
> Don't throw them away.
> Put them in the bottle bank.
> Recycle them today.
> For if ten green bottles
> Are not thrown away
> There'll be ten green bottles
> To use another day.

Conclusion
End with the slogans in 'Thought for the day'. Encourage the children to think up some other slogans of their own and to put them up around the school.

Thought for the day
Don't trash our future: Recycle.

> When you refuse to reuse,
> It's our Earth you abuse.

Just think before you bin it.
There could be some use in it.
Use it up. Wear it out.
Make it do, or do without.

WORLD WATER DAY

Aim
To make the children aware of the importance of having clean water and of the consequences of not having a supply of clean water.

Preparation
Infant classes can start thinking about why we need water and the importance of having clean water by singing the songs in *Wonderful Water* (Out of the Ark Music).

Invite a year 5 or year 6 class to think about people around the world who do not have a clean water supply. Encourage them to write a script that they can perform in the assembly which illustrates how not having clean water affects their lives. For example, they could role-play TV interviews with a number of people who do not have a clean water supply, such as someone living in a city which has become a war zone, a child living in a sub-Saharan village where the well has run dry, a child living in a slum in a city in India, or a child living in poverty in a remote village whose home has no toilet.

Prepare a number of statement cards giving facts about water to display around the school after the assembly. As well as the answers to the quiz you can include the following statements about water:

- Water is life. Clean water is not a luxury. Everyone has a right to a toilet.
- We should have showers instead of baths. Dirty water carries germs.

Introduction
Begin with these jokes about water.

Joke of the day
- What runs across the floor without any legs? Water.
- What is round and deep but could not be filled up by all the water in the world? A colander.
- What is full of holes but can still hold water? A sponge.

> Knock! Knock!
> Who's there?
> Water.
> Water who?
> Water is scarce, so don't waste it!

Explain that it is World Water Day.

Ask the children why we need to have a supply of clean water. Draw out points such as: for drinking; for cooking; for washing – ourselves, our clothes, our cooking utensils, our dishes; and for our toilets – to get rid of our waste. Point out that we also need water for our agriculture and our manufacturing industries.

Main focus: The importance of a clean water supply

A water quiz
Choose one or two people from each of the junior classes to take part in a quiz. Ask the contestants to stand in front of the audience and draw lots for the order in which they are to answer the questions. If they get a question right they are awarded a point; if they get it wrong they lose a point. The person with the most points at the end of the quiz is the winner. Ask a person from year 6 to keep the score.

Quiz questions:

1. How much of the Earth's surface is covered by water?
   More than half   Less than half
2. How much of the world's water is readily available for human use?
   98%   50%   10%   1%
3. How much of the human body consists of water?
   15%   30%   60%   70%

4. How long can a human being last without water?
   A few hours   A few days   2 or 3 weeks   A month
5. How many people in the world do not have access to safe, clean water?
   1 in 3   1 in 6   1 in 10   1 in 14
6. On average, how many children die each day from diarrhoea caused by dirty water and poor sanitation?
   300   900   1400   2600
7. Statement: More people in the world have mobile phones than have access to a toilet.
   True   False
8. How many hospital patients in developing countries are being treated for diseases caused by dirty water and poor sanitation?
   1 in 2   1 in 5   1 in 20   1 in 100
9. Which of these diseases is caused by a lack of clean water and poor sanitation?
   Dysentery   Diarrhoea   Cholera
10. What is the total of all the hours a year spent by women in sub-Saharan Africa collecting water?
    25,000   1 million   20 million   40 billion
11. How much money will provide someone in a developing country who does not have a clean water supply with clean water for life?
    £5   £15   £50

Answers: 1. More than half; 2. 1%; 3. 70%; 4. A few days; 5. 1 in 3; 6. 900; 7. True; 8. 1 in 2; 9. All three; 10. 40 billion; 11. £15.

Invite the class which has prepared a script to perform it. When they have finished, ask the rest of the children what they learned from the performance. Recap how different our lives would be without a clean water supply.

Conclusion
End with this World Water Day prayer:

> Let us pray for all those who do not have a clean water supply, for those who become ill from drinking dirty water and for those who face regular water shortages. May those of us

who have more than enough water recognise how fortunate we are and work together to help build a world in which everyone has access to enough clean water to meet their daily needs.

Thoughts for the day
Water is life and clean water means health.

Audrey Hepburn

Where there is water, people do not die.

African proverb

When the well dries, we know the wealth of water.

Benjamin Franklin

ZOO AWARENESS DAY

This day takes place on August 31.

Aim
To raise awareness of why we have zoos and issues about keeping animals in captivity.

Preparation
Encourage a class to prepare to present the arguments for and against keeping animals in zoos. Divide the class into two groups and invite one group to represent a pressure group called ZANY (Zoos Are Necessary) arguing why we should have zoos. The other group represents a pressure group called AKAZ (Against Keeping Animals in Zoos).

Encourage the children to think of how they can present the arguments; e.g. through interviews with people who agree with them. One group can prepare interviews with a zookeeper, a conservationist and a supporter of ZANY, while the other group can prepare interviews with an animals rights protester and a supporter of AKAZ. They can also include statements from animals;

e.g. an animal from an endangered species speaking in favour of zoos, and an animal who lives in a cage or enclosure that says it is very confining compared to where it would live in the wild. They can make masks for the animals which speak, and hold up posters presenting their arguments.

Introduction

Begin with a joke:

- What did Mrs Green ask Mrs Brown when Mrs Brown told her that she'd taken her son to the zoo? Answer: Did they accept him?

Ask the children to think about how they would feel if they were in a zoo and parties of animals came to look at them, and they only had the food and clothes that the keepers gave to them. Would it be like being in prison?

Explain that the assembly is going to focus on why we have zoos.

Main focus: Why do we have zoos?

Invite the class which has prepared the arguments for and against keeping animals in zoos to present their views. Then invite children from other classes to say what they think.

Draw two columns on the screen and list the arguments in favour of zoos in one column, then the arguments against zoos in the other column.

Finally, take a vote in which those who support zoos give them the thumbs up and those who are against them give them the thumbs down.

Read 'The Monkey'. Ask: What message do you think the poet is trying to give in the poem? Why does he say the monkey is more skilful than any acrobat? What does he suggest is the monkey's attitude to visitors? What does he suggest the monkey would do if it was returned to the forest?

The Monkey
> More skilful
> Than any acrobat,
> The monkey
> Swings himself
> Across the cage.
> Then sits, bored,
> Staring at the visitors
> Who offer food
> He does not need
> And urge him
> To perform tricks
> He does not want to do.
>
> What a performance
> He would give them
> In the forest's trees,
> If only he were there.

Conclusion
End with the thought for the day.

Thought for the day
> People forget the good that zoos do. If it weren't for zoos we
> would have so many species that would be extinct today.
>
> Betty White

CHAPTER 4

Festivals and celebrations

BONFIRE NIGHT

Aim
To explain why we celebrate Bonfire Night and to stress the dangers of fireworks and the need to follow the Firework Code.

Preparation
Ask a class to prepare a presentation on firework safety which explains the firework safety code. Encourage them to research what the code says, then to think of how they might present the information through role-plays or interviews in which they show the consequences of not adhering to the code, and true stories of accidents that occurred because people ignored the advice given in the code.

The class can make posters about each piece of advice in the Firework Code to hold up after the presentation to reinforce the messages contained in the code.

The Firework Code
- Keep pets indoors.
- Don't give sparklers to very young children.
- Wear gloves when holding a sparkler.
- Don't touch a sparkler when it's gone out. Put it in a bucket of water.
- Don't light fireworks. Leave it to adults.
- Stand well back.
- Don't go near a firework that has been lit but hasn't gone off.
- Do not play with fireworks and never throw them.

Introduction

Explain that the theme of the assembly is to explore why we have fireworks on November 5 and to consider how dangerous fireworks are.

Main focus: Why we celebrate Guy Fawkes Night

Start with a Question and Answer session in which you interview another teacher and ask the questions and they give the answers.

Q. Why is November 5 Bonfire Night?

A. Because of the Gunpowder Plot.

Q. Why was it called the Gunpowder Plot?

A. Because on November 5 1605 a group of men, which included someone called Guy Fawkes, planned to blow up Parliament using barrels of gunpowder which they put in a cellar underneath the Parliament building.

Q. Why did they want to blow up Parliament?

A. Because King James I was a Protestant and they were Catholics.

Q. What happened?

A. The plot was discovered and Guy Fawkes was arrested and put to death.

Q. Some people want fireworks to be banned. Why?

A. Because fireworks are dangerous and every year about 1,300 people are injured in the four weeks around Bonfire Night – about half of them children.

Q. Why are they dangerous?

A. Because they contain gunpowder, which is explosive. Because they create so much heat – three sparklers create as much heat as a blowtorch. And because they travel so fast – a rocket can travel at 150 miles per hour.

Q. What sort of injuries do they cause?

A. Burns and scars. They can damage your eyes. People have been maimed and blinded.

Q. How can accidents be avoided?

A. By never playing with fireworks and following the Firework Code.

Next, ask the class to do the presentation that they have prepared, ending with the display of posters.

Then read this poem:

Guy Fawkes Day Incident
    'I didn't mean to do it.
    It slipped from my hand as I threw it,'
    Tom splutters, his face streaked with tears.

    He sees again Sandra's look of surprise
    As the firework struck her cheek.

    He hears again Sandra's scream of terror
    As the firework exploded.

    'Will it leave a scar?' he asks.

    'The doctor said it's too early to tell
    How scarred she'll be,'
    Says his mother, sighing.

    'I didn't mean to do it.
    It slipped from my hand as I threw it,'
    Tom splutters, his face streaked with tears.

Explain that it is an offence to throw a firework in a public place.

Conclusion
End by reminding the children of the Firework Code.

Thought for the day
Firework slogans:

- Never handle a Roman candle.
- Anyone who fools with fireworks is crackers.
- Don't be a jerk. Never play with a firework.

Follow-up activity
Encourage the children to make 'Wanted' posters for Guy Fawkes.

Further resources
Liveleak.com has a very powerful 10-second video which shows a boy trying to throw a firework which explodes in his face. (You do not see his face, but you hear his screams.)

CHINESE NEW YEAR

Aim
To understand when and how Chinese New Year is celebrated.

Preparation
At the Chinese New Year one custom is to put short poems giving messages of goodwill on doors. The poems are written on red paper, as red represents good luck and good fortune in Chinese culture.

Examples are:

- May the stars shine upon you and bring you wealth, happiness and health.
- Be patient though the road may bend. Good fortune awaits you at the end.

Encourage the children to write messages to put on the doors around the school. Some of them can read out the messages in the assembly.

The children can also be involved in preparing a procession to begin the assembly. They could make dragon masks or alternatively they could make a model dragon to lead the procession followed by other children who could recite the poem (below) while wearing or holding dragon masks.

Chinese music that can be played while the children are entering the hall can be found on YouTube; e.g. search for 'Happy Chinese Music' or 'Chinese New Year Music'. Songs to listen to are: 'Chinese New Year Song' by The Kiboomers and 'What's Your Zodiac Sign?' by Dream English Kids.

Introduction

Read the poem 'Chinese New Year Dragon'. Then explain that the dragon dance is part of the procession that takes place on Chinese New Year. In Chinese legends the dragon is a friendly, helpful creature. The dragon is a symbol of wisdom, power and wealth and is believed to drive away evil spirits and bad luck. Music for the dance is provided by horns, gongs and drums. The dragon is held up on poles which are moved up and down to make it sway and dance.

Chinese New Year Dragon
>   There's a brightly coloured dragon
>   Swaying down the street,
>   Stomping and stamping
>   And kicking up its feet.
>
>   There's a multi-coloured dragon –
>   Green, gold and red –
>   Twisting and twirling
>   And shaking its head.
>
>   There's a silky-scaled dragon
>   Parading through the town,
>   Swishing and swooshing
>   And rippling up and down.

There's a swirling, whirling dragon,
Weaving to and fro,
Prancing and dancing
And putting on a show.

There's cheering and clapping
As the dragon draws near –
A sign of good luck
And a happy New Year!

Main focus: The 12 animals of the Chinese zodiac

Explain that each year in the Chinese calendar is named after an animal. The 12 animals are used in this order: Rat, Ox, Tiger, Rabbit, Dragon, Snake, Horse, Sheep, Monkey, Rooster, Dog, Pig.

Put the order up on the screen. Explain that 2018 is the Year of the Dog, 2019 the Year of the Pig and 2020 the Year of the Rat.

According to legend, the animals took part in a great race and the first 12 to finish were chosen.

Read the poem below, which explains how Rat came in first and why Cat failed to finish in the first 12.

The Rat and the Cat
The cat said to his friend the rat,
'Have you heard the exciting news?
Each year is to have an animal's name
Which the Emperor will choose.'

'I'd like a year named after me,'
Said Rat, and Cat said, 'I would too.
But every animal would like that,
So here's what we must do.'

'We must get up very early,'
The cat said, and he gave a yawn.
'So wake me up in the morning
And we'll set off long before dawn.'

Rat was so excited that he forgot
His promise to wake the cat.
He was dreaming of the first year
Being called the Year of the Rat.

The other animals were still getting ready
When Rat set off down the track.
But he could see them catching up
Whenever he looked back.

The tiger was roaring. The dog was barking.
The monkey swung by on a tree.
'If I don't do something fast,' Rat thought,
'They'll all get there before me.'

So Rat went to the ox and said,
'If you let me ride on your back
I will sing to you as you run
And make sure you follow the track.'

As Rat sang, the ox ran so fast
He left all the others behind.
The ox thought he'd come in first
But he was amazed to find

That the rat had slid off his back
And crossed the finishing line
So the Emperor gave the rat
The prize of the first sign.

When the cat finally arrived
He was too late to be given a sign.
Which is why the cat hates the rat
And chases him all the time.

Conclusion

End by asking some of the children to read the messages of good-will that they have written.

Further resources
Facts about Chinese New Year can be given in a PowerPoint presentation, such as 'The Chinese New Year' (www.primaryworks.co.uk).

A video, suitable for infants, which introduces the 12 animals of the Chinese zodiac and tells the story of how the animals got years named after them is available at www.bbc.co.uk/Cbeebies/stories/lets-celebrate-chinesenewyearperformance.

CHRISTMAS

Aim
To understand the importance of Christmas for Christians, and how it is celebrated in different countries.

Preparation
Encourage each class to prepare to contribute a short item to the assembly focussed on a part of the Christmas story. For example, a class might focus on the journey to Bethlehem with an interviewer asking Joseph and Mary to explain where they are going and why, or may act out a scene involving the shepherds or the three wise men.

Download a PowerPoint presenting the story of the Nativity, such as that produced by Primary Works.

Set up a Nativity scene on a display table in the hall, so that the children can refer to it after the assembly.

Prepare these songs for the children to sing at the beginning and end of the assembly: 'We Wish You a Merry Christmas' by Warrell and 'Merry Christmas Everybody' by Slade.

Introduction
Explain that the focus of the assembly is on the Christian celebration of the birth of Jesus on December 25 and that during the assembly you are going to tell the story of the Nativity.

Main focus: The story of the Nativity
Tell the story of the Nativity, putting up the slides of the PowerPoint as appropriate and incorporating the items which each class has prepared.

The Christmas message
Talk about what Christmas means to Christians and how it is more than giving and receiving presents and families getting together and having parties. For Christians it is a time of peace and goodwill when they go to church and donate money to charities.

Conclusion
Ask: If you had three Christmas wishes for the world, what would they be? Then end by reading the poem 'If I Had Three Christmas Wishes' followed by the Christmas prayer.

If I Had Three Christmas Wishes
>   If I had three Christmas wishes
>   My first wish would be
>   For an end to hunger and poverty.
>
>   If I had three Christmas wishes
>   My second would be for
>   An end to violence, hatred and war.
>
>   If I had three Christmas wishes
>   My third wish would be
>   That we take proper care of the land and the sea.

A Christmas prayer
>   As we celebrate Christmas, sharing presents and foods with our families, let us remember those less fortunate than us who have been forced from their homes by war or famine and those who are too poor to be able to celebrate as we do.
>   Let us remember too those who do not celebrate Christmas, because their religion is different from ours, and let us live together in peace respecting and tolerating each other.

May we set aside our differences and work together to look after the world and take care of the land and the sea and all the creatures with whom we share our planet.

May we look towards the future unselfishly and with hope.

DIVALI

Aim
To understand what happens at the Hindu festival of Divali.

Preparation
Encourage classes to research the story of Rama and Sita. One class could make puppets, which they could use to retell the story in assembly. The puppets can be simple cards fixed to sticks or more elaborate ones using different coloured fabrics.

Introduction
Explain that Divali is a Hindu festival that takes place in October or November. It is known as the festival of lights and celebrates the triumph of good over evil, of light over darkness and of knowledge over ignorance. Talk about how Divali is the festival of lights and explain how Hindus make patterns with coloured powders on the floors of their homes.

Main focus: Celebrating Divali
Read the poem below and talk about how it describes how Hindus celebrate Divali:

It's Divali Tonight
Everything's ready to greet the new year.
Everything's bright with light.
Everyone's dressed up and full of joy.
It's Divali tonight!

We've lit the lamps to show the way
Up to our front door.

We've sprinkled coloured powders
To make pictures on the floor.

We've given each other gifts of sweets.
There's lots of delicious things to eat.

Everything's ready to greet the new year.
Everything's bright with light.
Everyone's dressed up and full of joy.
It's Divali tonight!

The story of Rama and Sita

Explain that at Divali Hindus also remember the story of Rama and Sita.

Either ask the class who have made the puppets to tell the story of
Rama and Sita or read the story (below).

The Legend of Rama and Sita

Long ago there was a prince called Rama who was the son of a
great king. Everyone expected that Rama would become king
when his father died. But his stepmother wanted her son to
become king. So she tricked the king into sending Rama and
his wife, the beautiful princess Sita, into exile.

They made their home in a forest. But the forest was full of evil
demons. One of the demons was Ravanna, who had 20 arms
and 10 heads. When he saw Sita he planned to kidnap her and
take her to live with him on the island of Sri Lanka. He used a
beautiful deer to lure Sita away from Rama, then flew down in
a chariot pulled by flying monsters and captured her.

Sita was very frightened, but she was clever. As she was a princess, she wore lots of jewels. One by one she dropped the pieces of
jewellery to form a trail showing where Ravanna was taking her.

Rama was determined to free Sita, so he enlisted the help of
Hanuman the monkey king. Hanuman flew to find out where
Sita was being held. Then he raised a great army of monkeys,
bears and other animals. The animals formed a bridge so that
Rama could cross to the island where Sita was.

Then they fought a great battle with the demons. They freed Sita and she and Rama set off to return to claim the kingdom from which they had been banished.

Darkness fell before they reached the kingdom, so the people there lit torches and lamps to show them the way into the city. And Rama became king and Sita became queen.

Today, Hindus set lights outside their homes and in their windows remembering the story of Rama and Sita.

Conclusion
End with these two prayers for Divali.

Prayers for Divali
> O Lord, lead me from darkness to light, and from death to immortality.
> Let there be peace, peace and real peace.
>
> Candles of hope burning bright.
> May our festival of light
> Banish ignorance and fear
> And bring us peace throughout the year.

Thought for the day
> On this auspicious festival of light,
> may the glow of joy,
> prosperity and happiness
> illuminate your life and your home.

Divali greetings card

Further resources
A PowerPoint presentation explaining what Divali is and telling the story of Rama and Sita can found at the TES resources website.

A PDF containing a series of images of Divali can be obtained from the Assembly Box website. There is also a detailed plan for an assembly on Hindu festivals throughout the year.

EID AL-ADHA

Aim

To understand what the festival of Eid al-Adha is and how Muslims celebrate it.

Preparation

Prepare to play one or two of the songs for Eid which can be found on YouTube. You can play them as the children file in to the assembly.

Introduction

Invite the children to wish each other a happy Eid by saying 'Eid Mubarak' to each other. Explain that 'Eid Mubarak' means 'Have a blessed festival.' They can respond to the greeting by saying 'Khair Mubarak', which wishes goodwill to the person who greeted them, or 'Jazek Allah Khair', which translates as 'May Allah reward you with goodness.'

Main focus: The festival of Eid al-Adha

Explain that Eid al-Adha is also known as the festival of sacrifice.

Read this poem:

On This Day
> On this day
> We remember how Allah tested Ibrahim
> By demanding that he sacrifice his son.
> The devil tempted Ibrahim
> To defy Allah
> But Ibrahim did not give in
> To temptation.
> So Allah told Ibrahim
> He could sacrifice a lamb instead.

Explain that Muslims celebrate Eid al-Adha by dressing in their best clothes and going to the mosque to pray. Then family and friends give each other gifts. They also give money and gifts to the poor so that they can join in and celebrate too.

Conclusion

End with this prayer:

Today I pray that
Happiness be at your door.
May it knock early
Stay late and leave the gifts of Allah's
Peace, joy, love and good health behind.
Shaban Mubarak, Eid Mubarak, Ramadan Mubarak.
May you remain happy all the time
Irrespective of any occasion.

Thought for the day

My wish for you on this Eid.
May peace and joy embrace your life
And stay on this blessed day and always.

Eid greeting

EID AL-FITR

Aim

To help the children to understand why Muslims fast during Ramadan and how they celebrate Eid al-Fitr at the end of Ramadan.

Preparation

Invite a class to research what Ramadan is and why Muslims fast during Ramadan, and to write and perform a script to explain why Ramadan is an important time for Muslims and what happens at Eid al-Fitr.

Prepare to play a song for Eid, such as the 'Song for Eid' uploaded by Appuseries which can be found on YouTube.

Introduction

Ask the children whether they have ever been sponsored to go without a meal in order to raise money to provide for people less fortunate than themselves who may be unable to get enough to eat. How easy would it be to go without food for a whole day? Explain that going without food is called fasting and that Muslims fast during the hours of daylight during the holy month of Ramadan, and explain the purpose of the assembly.

Main focus
Ask the children who have prepared the script to present it.

Put the video of the 'Song for Eid' upon the screen and invite the children to join in and sing it.

Invite a local imam or a senior member of the Muslim community to come into the assembly and be interviewed by the children. Prepare the children for the visit by getting them to write questions they would like answered.

Conclusion
End with this prayer:

> We pray for those who are fasting during Ramadan.
> Give them the strength to deny all the needs of their bodies.
> Help them to draw closer to Allah.
> Help them to grow in compassion
> for those in the world who are hungry
> and less fortunate than themselves.

Further resources
A PowerPoint presentation about Ramadan and Eid al-Fitr can be obtained from www.primaryworks.co.uk.

GURU NANAK'S BIRTHDAY

Aim
To explain how Sikhs celebrate Guru Nanak's Birthday.

Preparation
Prepare some examples of Sikh music from www.YouTube.com/user/SikhMusic to play while the children are entering and leaving the hall.

Obtain images of Sikhs and gurdwara from www.dreamstime.com to provide a slideshow to accompany your explanations in the main part of the assembly.

Introduction

Explain that the focus of the assembly is on the birthday of Guru Nanak, the founder of the Sikh religion, and how it is celebrated. The exact date varies but comes around the beginning of November.

Main focus: How Sikhs celebrate Guru Nanak's Birthday

Ask another teacher to act as an expert on Sikhism and present the facts about the celebrations in the form of an interview. Alternatively, if there are any children from Sikh families, you can invite them or members of their families to be interviewed and to answer the questions. Put up appropriate slides to accompany each question.

Q. Why do Sikhs celebrate Guru Nanak's Birthday?

A. Because Guru Nanak was the founder of Sikhism, which is based on Guru Nanak's teachings as recorded in the holy book the Guru Granth Sahib.

Q. Do Sikhs have a religious ceremony to celebrate his birthday?

A. They celebrate by having a team of people who spend the two days before his actual birthday reading aloud the holy book. They end early on the morning of his birthday.

Q. What happens next?

A. They go to the Sikh temple, which is called a gurdwara.

Q. I heard that in some places they organise processions. Is that right?

A. Yes, there are processions in some parts of India and in parts of England too. They are led by people who represent the followers of Guru Nanak and there are singers and musicians and even teams of people demonstrating martial arts.

Q. Do they decorate the gurdwara in any way?

A. Yes, they put up lights and flags and decorate it with flowers.

Q. Do they have a religious ceremony?

A. Yes, they start early in the morning singing hymns, reciting poems and praying.

Q. Does everyone then go home for an exchange of gifts and a family meal?

A. No, they all eat together in the gurdwara. A sweet made from semolina or flour, sugar and ghee (a sort of butter) is blessed and shared. Then everyone has a meal made in the free kitchen. They are following what Guru Nanak taught, that everyone is equal and you should share with anyone less fortunate than you.

Q. What if there are people who are unable to go to the gurdwara? What do they do?

A. They celebrate by holding a similar ceremony at home.

Q. And after the meal, is there anything else?

A. The celebrations may go on until late at night and may end with fireworks.

Note: If the interviewee is a Sikh, you can then invite questions from the children.

Read this poem:

On Guru Nanak's Birthday
　　On Guru Nanak's Birthday
　　Hear what he had to say.
　　No one is greater than another.
　　Every person is your brother.
　　Share with them your hopes and fears.
　　Share your laughter and your tears.

Share your riches and possessions.
So join your neighbours in processions
To the holy temple where
There's a lunch for all to share.

Conclusion
End with this thought for the day.

Thought for the day
Let us follow Guru Nanak's teaching
By sharing with others,
By helping those who have less than us and are in need,
By being honest and truthful in our dealings with others.

HANUKKAH

Aim
To tell the story of Hanukkah and how it is celebrated by Jews throughout the world.

Preparation
Prepare to play one of the several videos that can be found on YouTube telling the story of Hanukkah. There are also several Hanukkah songs that you can play, such as 'Hanukkah! Oh Hanukkah!' and 'Dreidel, Dreidel, Dreidel', available with lyrics from www.learningstationmusic.com.

If possible, borrow a dreidel to show to the children, and invite a rabbi or another member of the local Jewish community to participate in the assembly by telling the story of Hanukkah.

Introduction
Show the children a dreidel or put up a picture of one. Ask: Does anyone know what this is? Ask anyone who answers if they know how to use it. Explain how Jews play games with it at Hanukkah, which is the Jewish festival of lights. Talk about how Jews celebrate

the eight days of Hanukkah by lighting a candle in each of the candlesticks on the eight days that Hanukkah lasts. Explain that during Hanukkah Jews exchange gifts and eat special foods, just as Christians do at Christmas and Muslims do at Eid.

Main focus: The story of Hanukkah
Use the video that you have found to tell the story of Hanukkah.

Conclusion
Invite the children to sing 'Dreidel, Dreidel, Dreidel' by playing the song and putting the lyrics up on the screen.

End with these two messages from Hanukkah greetings cards:

- May you be blessed with joy, good health, peace and all the best things that life brings.
- May the season of beauty and light fill your heart and home with happiness.

Follow-up activities
Encourage the children to make dreidels and to play the game using either counters or chocolate coins. There is a Wikihow video which shows how to make a paper dreidel, and a video explaining how to play the game.

HARVEST FESTIVAL

Aim
To celebrate the gathering in of the harvest and to think about sharing.

Preparation
Collect donations of produce that can be displayed in the hall before either giving it to a local food bank or a charity, such as the Salvation Army, to distribute.

Invite a class to prepare a presentation of the poem 'Harvest Time'. Encourage them to think of actions that they can perform to accompany the verses.

Prepare to play a harvest festival song from YouTube, e.g. 'Harvest Samba' or 'Let's Harvest' (a song by Al Start).

Harvest Time
> Harvest time! Harvest time!
> It's harvest time again.
> Time to cut the corn
> And gather in the grain.
>
> Harvest time! Harvest time!
> Time to pick the fruits,
> To gather in the nuts
> And dig up all the roots.
>
> Harvest time! Harvest time!
> In the autumn sun
> We'll cut, pick and dig
> Until the harvest's done.

Introduction
Ask the class to present the poem, and talk about all the things that are mentioned in it.

Talk about how traditionally after the harvest was completed a harvest supper would be held as well as a harvest thanksgiving in church.

Main focus: Sharing
Explain that harvest festival is a time when we share our food with others, and that sharing can sometimes be difficult. For example, you may have to let someone else have the last biscuit or the last sweet. Encourage the children to think about who they would

share their last bar of chocolate with. Invite some children to say who they would share it with.

Then, ask the children: If you and another child of your age were refugees and were starving, what would you do if you were given an apple? Would you share it? Ask for a show of hands. Ask: Would you keep it all for yourself or share it? Would it make a difference if the child was your brother or sister? Or if the child was a friend? Or if the child was from a different racial or religious background?

Emphasise that sharing isn't always easy and that we sometimes have to make difficult decisions depending on the circumstances.

Conclusion
Invite the children to join in singing the harvest festival song that you found on YouTube.

Explain which charity the food that has been donated is going to, and end with this harvest prayer:

A Harvest Prayer
As we celebrate and give thanks for our harvest,
Let us remember others less fortunate than us
Who do not have enough to eat,
Who are hungry and starving
Because of war and famine.
Let us send them sacks of grain
And share our harvest with them
For they are our brothers and sisters.

Thought for the day
Harvest isn't just the act of picking a vegetable from the vine; it is the season for collecting the crops and celebrating the plentiful gifts our garden has brought to us.

NATIONAL PETS DAY

Aim
To understand what pets need and the responsibilities a pet owner has.

Preparation
Invite a class to think about the responsibilities you have if you own a pet. Get them to list the responsibilities and to make a placard for each one. They can work out a script listing the responsibilities and hold up the placards in turn. Below is a list of the responsibilities they should include:

- Feed your pet regularly.
- Make sure it always has water to drink.
- Give it a suitable diet.
- Don't give it too many treats.
- Don't overfeed it.
- Provide it with a suitable bed or home.
- Clean up after it.
- Ensure it gets enough exercise.
- Train it.
- Play with it.
- Give it regular health checks.
- Take it to a vet if it is ill.
- Keep it under control.
- Don't let it annoy neighbours.

Introduction
Introduce the assembly by telling the children that it is National Pets Day. Ask: At what age can you buy a pet? Explain that the age used to be 12 but was recently raised to 16. Ask: What do you think was the reason for raising the age? Do you think the government were right to raise the age?

Main Focus: Pets and their needs
Ask them to think about their pets and what their pet needs. What does a dog need? A cat need? A gerbil need? A hamster need?

Write a list of their suggestions on the board – food, water, shelter, somewhere to keep warm, enough space to move around, plenty of exercise.

Then read this poem:

I'm a Pet Rabbit
> I'm a pet rabbit. I don't have much.
> My life is spent here in this hutch.
> I've plenty of food and straw in my home.
> But I wish I'd a burrow and fields to roam.
>
> I'm a pet rabbit. You look after me
> But I'm trapped in this cage.
> And I long to be free.

Ask: Is the rabbit in the poem having its needs met? Do the pets that you know have their needs met? Think of a particular pet. If it could speak, what would it have to say about its needs? What is the thing it would like to have most because it would improve its life?

Invite the class to perform the presentation they have prepared about the responsibilities of owning a pet.

Conclusion
End with this prayer for pets:

A Prayer for Pets
> Good St Francis, you loved all of God's creatures. To you they were your brothers and sisters. Help us to follow your example of treating every living thing with kindness. St Francis, patron saint of animals, watch over my pet and keep my companion safe and healthy. Amen.

Thoughts for the day
When you have a pet, you make a commitment to look after it properly.

A person who is cruel to a pet should be ashamed of themselves.

NATIONAL POETRY DAY

National Poetry Day is usually held in October.

Aim
To share favourite poems and to say why they are favourites.

Preparation
Invite both the children and all the adults who work in the school – the teachers and teaching assistants, the secretary, the dinner ladies and canteen staff, the caretaker and cleaners – and other adults who are connected with the school, e.g. the governors and parents, to choose a favourite poem that they would like to share in the assembly. You could also ask them to make a copy of the poem, which you can put on display around the school.

Ask the children and those adults who can attend the assembly to write their names and the name of the poem on a slip of paper and to put the slip into a hat.

Note: If you organise a poetry-speaking competition (see below) you will need to purchase poetry books as prizes and prepare certificates for the runners-up.

Introduction
Explain that it is National Poetry Day and tell them about events that are taking place to celebrate it.

Main focus: Sharing poems
Hold a sharing assembly in which you draw slips of paper from the hat and the child or adult whose name is drawn out shares their poem and says why they like it.

Alternatively, the assembly could come at the end of a poetry week and could be the culmination of a poetry-speaking competition involving all the children. Each child could learn a poem to recite to their class. Two or more winners could be chosen from each class to present their poems in the assembly, with the overall winner and runners-up chosen in the assembly. The prizes could be poetry books, and each person who recited a poem in the assembly could receive a certificate.

Classes could also be asked to take part in a choral-speaking competition in which each class learns and performs a poem in the assembly. There could also be a competition for the adults to learn and perform a poem.

Use the poem 'Climb Aboard the Poetry Plane' at either the beginning or end of the assembly and ask: What does the poem say about the different ways that poetry can stimulate your imagination and stir your emotions?

Climb Aboard the Poetry Plane
> Climb aboard the poetry plane
> And speed across the sky.
> Visit worlds of wonder
> Let your imagination fly.
>
> Circle castles in the clouds.
> Watch mermaids flick their tails.
> Hear the mighty dragons roar
> And shake their shimmering scales.
>
> Feel the flickerings of hope.
> Taste anger's bitter tear.
> Creep inside the monster's heart
> And share his shivering fear.
>
> Smell the scent of the wild rose.
> Snorkel in coral seas.
> Dance on the deck of a rainbow.
> Float on the fluttering breeze.
>
> Climb aboard the poetry plane
> And speed across the sky.
> Visit worlds of wonder
> Let your imagination fly.

Thought for the day
A poem is like a painting in words.

Anon

REMEMBRANCE DAY

Aim
To understand why November 11 is Remembrance Day and how the poppy became a symbol of remembrance.

Preparation
Prepare to show the animation telling the story of the poppy and how it became a symbol of remembrance from the British Legion website, www.britishlegion.org.uk. Ask one of the children to prepare a reading of the poem 'In Flanders Fields'.

Prepare a recording of a bugler playing 'The Last Post'. You could also play, as appropriate, 'It's a Long Way to Tipperary' and 'Abide With Me'.

Introduction
Explain the aim of the assembly. Ask: What do you know about the First World War? When did it take place? Who fought in it? Is there a war memorial in the city, town or village where you live? Whose names are on it? Does anyone lay a wreath on it in November each year?

Explain that November 11 is Remembrance Day, when we remember the soldiers who died in the First World War. It is held on November 11 because in 1918 the First World War ended on the eleventh hour of the eleventh day of the eleventh month. It is known as Armistice Day.

A two-minute silence is held throughout the country at 11.00 am on November 11 in memory of those who were died. People wear poppies as a symbol of remembrance.

Main focus: How the poppy became a symbol of remembrance

Use the British Legion's animation to tell the story of how the poppy became a symbol of remembrance. Put a copy of 'In Flanders Fields' on the screen and ask one of the children to read it.

In Flanders Fields

In Flanders fields the poppies blow
Between the crosses, row on row,
That mark our place; and in the sky
The larks, still bravely singing, fly
Scarce heard amid the guns below.

We are the Dead. Short days ago
We lived, felt dawn, saw sunset glow,
Loved and were loved, and now we lie
In Flanders fields.

Take up our quarrel with the foe:
To you from failing hands we throw
The torch; be yours to hold it high.
If ye break faith with us who die
We shall not sleep, though poppies grow
In Flanders fields.

John McCrae

Conclusion

Explain that Remembrance Sunday is the second Sunday in November, when there is a parade of veterans and wreaths are laid at the Cenotaph in London. On Remembrance Sunday we remember the sacrifice not only of those who died in the First World War, but of everyone who has died in the two world wars and other conflicts such as the Falklands War and the war in Afghanistan in order to protect our freedom.

Thought for the day

Greater love hath no man than this that he lay down his life for his friends.

The Bible, John 15:13

When you go home
Tell them of us and say
For your tomorrow
We gave our today.

Attributed to John Maxwell Edmonds

They fell but o'er their glorious grave
Floats free the banner of the cause they died to save.

Francis Marion Crawford

Further resources

The British Legion has produced learning packs about Remembrance Day. Details can be found at www.britishlegion.org.uk. A scripted assembly for Remembrance Day is available at www.assemblies. org.uk.

ST ANDREW'S DAY

Aim

To explain how St Andrew became the patron saint of Scotland and how St Andrew's Day is celebrated.

Preparation

Children can make copies of the Scottish flag – a white cross on a blue background, known as a saltire – to bring into the assembly. A junior class could make a large flag and process into the assembly behind a standard-bearer, while a recording of 'Scotland the Brave' or 'Flower of Scotland' is being played on bagpipes.

Find images of tartans, Scots in kilts and pipers and pipe bands and put them on the whiteboard. Prepare recordings of pipe bands playing tunes such as 'Flower of Scotland', 'Auld Lang Syne', 'The Skye Boat Song' and 'The Bonnie Banks o' Loch Lomond'.

Introduction

Explain that many countries have a patron saint – a saint with a particular connection with the country, who looks after and protects the people of that country.

Talk about how St Andrew is the patron saint of Scotland and explain that November 30 is St Andrew's Day and is a national holiday in Scotland.

Main focus: How St Andrew became the patron saint of Scotland

Put the poem below on the screen and discuss what it says about how St Andrew became the patron saint of Scotland.

How St Andrew Became the Patron Saint of Scotland
    Through the towns and villages of Scotland
    The story is still told
    Of how King Angus raised an army
    Of Scotsmen brave and bold
    To fight the Anglo-Saxons
    Led by King Athelstan
    And of the vision that Angus had
    Before the battle began
    Of a white cross in the clear blue sky
    When he knelt down to pray
    That showed St Andrew would help the Scots
    To win the fight that day.
    So King Angus made a promise
    That St Andrew should be
    The patron saint of Scotland
    Following the Scots' victory.
    And King Angus kept his promise
    And the white cross on the blue
    Known as the saltire also became
    The flag of Scotland too.

Talk about how people celebrate St Andrew's Day. They put the Scottish flag in their windows and outside their homes. They wear tartan clothes and take part in processions.

Put up images of tartans, of Scots wearing kilts and of pipe bands on the screen, while explaining that tartan is a pattern made by inter-weaving horizontal and vertical bands of colour. Originally tartans were woollen, but nowadays other materials are used as well.

Talk about how in the past there were different family groups or clans who ruled in different areas of Scotland. Each clan had its own tartan. Today, people who can trace their ancestry back to a particular clan wear kilts and other clothes, such as plaids – a sort of blanket worn over the shoulder – in the tartan of their clan.

Sing a Scottish song. Put the words of the song on the screen.

Conclusion
End with a St Andrew's Day prayer:

> On this St Andrew's Day
> We pray for all Scottish people:
> Those who were born in Scotland,
> Those who have left to live abroad,
> And those who have made Scotland their home.
> May the people of Scotland
> Work together for the common good
> And use their talents to create a better world.

Further resources
For detailed ideas for an assembly about St Andrew, focussing on the theme of loyalty, see the Assembly Box website.

ST DAVID'S DAY

Aim
To understand who St David was and how the Welsh celebrate St David's Day.

Preparation
Classes can prepare for the St David's Day assembly by researching famous men and women from Wales, such as the politician David Lloyd George, who was Prime Minister from 1916–1922; poet Dylan Thomas; Labour politician Aneurin Bevan; Paralympic gold medallist Dame Tanni Grey-Thompson; singers Dame Shirley

Bassey and Tom Jones; footballer Gareth Bale; and rugby player Sam Warburton. They could produce mini-biographies for individuals to present in the assembly.

Prepare some traditional harp music to play as the children enter the hall.

Introduction

Explain that St David is the patron saint of Wales and that March 1 is St David's Day.

Main focus: What it means to be Welsh

Put up a map of the United Kingdom and point out where Wales is.

Ask the children questions about Wales and what it means to be Welsh:

- What do you think of when someone says the name of the country Wales? Daffodils and leeks? Rugby union and football? Choirs and singing?
- What does it mean to be Welsh? That you live in Wales? That you were born in Wales? That your parents were born in Wales? That your grandparents were born in Wales? That you speak the Welsh language?

Explain that one of the stories told about St David is of how he helped the Welsh to a victory over the Saxons by getting them to wear leeks to enable them to tell friend from foe. The story explains how the leek became a symbol of Wales.

Put this poem on the screen and read it:

On St David's Day
> Today's St David's Day and throughout Wales
> They'll tell again the tales
> Of how in days of old St David told
> The Celtic warriors how they might

Tell friend from enemy in the fight
To save their lands
From falling into Saxon hands.
'Put leeks in your caps so that we'll know
Who is friend and who is foe.'
And so the leek has come to be
A symbol of Wales that you will see
Being worn by proud Welshmen today
Because today's St David's Day.

The children can then read any mini-biographies of famous Welsh
people that they have written. Afterwards they can put them
together as a booklet, which can go in the library.

Conclusion
The whole school can then sing the St David's Day anthem written
by singer Gwenno, which is available on YouTube and is sung all
over the world on St David's Day.

Thought for the day
End the assembly with this prayer for St David's Day written by the
Archbishop of Wales, the Most Revd Dr Barry Morgan:

God our Father
You called your servant David to uphold the Christian faith
amongst the people of Wales,
to encourage them by his observation of fasting and obedience,
and to show them compassion through small acts of great
love.
As light is poured onto the mountain-tops and as fresh rain is
sprinkled on the hills,
help us to be good carers of one another and of Your great and
glorious Creation.

Further resources
Further information about St David can be given in a PowerPoint
about him available from www.primaryworks.co.uk.

ST GEORGE'S DAY

Aim
To retell the story of St George and the dragon and to help the children to understand who St George was and what is known about his life.

Preparation
Prepare a recording of Elgar's 'Pomp and Circumstance March No 1' to play as the children enter the hall.

Invite classes to research the legend of St George and the dragon and choose one class to script a performance in which they present the story as part of the assembly. A version of the story can be found at http://images.scholastic.co.uk.

Make some A4 size cards with *TRUE* or *FALSE* on them. You will need enough for each of the class or house representatives to have the two different cards. Also, make some numbered cards from 0–10 so that each of the scorers has a set (see the quiz below).

Introduction
Introduce the assembly by explaining that April 23 is St George's Day and that St George is the patron saint of England and that he is famous for slaying the dragon. Then either ask the class which has prepared a performance of the story to present it or use a version of the story (see above) and tell it to pupils.

Main focus: A St George's Day quiz
Choose two representatives from each class – one to be the contestant, one to be the scorer. Explain that you are going to read out 10 statements about St George and that the contestants have to decide whether the statement is true or false and hold up the appropriate card. You then give the answer and each person who answered correctly scores a point for their class. After each question the scorer holds up the score for their class.

- Q1. St George was an Englishman. *(False – he was born in Turkey.)*
- Q2. St George was a Roman soldier. *(True.)*
- Q3. St George came to England when the Romans invaded England. *(False – St George never came to England.)*
- Q4. St George was a Christian. *(True.)*
- Q5. St George was a martyr. (Explain what being a martyr means.) *(True – he was tortured and executed in 303 AD.)*
- Q6. St George became the patron saint of England in Queen Victoria's reign. *(False – he became England's patron saint in medieval times.)*
- Q7. St George was admired for his bravery and courage and is the patron saint of other countries besides England. *(True.)*
- Q8. The story of St George and the dragon is a true story. It happened in Libya. *(False.)*
- Q9. On St George's Day some English people wear a red rose. *(True – the red rose is worn as a symbol by some people.)*
- Q10. St George was adopted as the patron saint of scouting by its founder. (Explain what scouting is.) *(True – the founder of scouting, Lord Baden-Powell, adopted St George as a symbol of faith, perseverance and courage.)*

Conclusion
End with the thought for the day.

Thought for the day
Let us remember St George as a person worthy of being a patron saint – for the bravery he showed in the face of persecution, for his refusal to give up his faith and the courage with which he met his death.

Further resources
A PowerPoint presentation telling the story of St George is available from www.tes.com. An audio version of the story can be found at www.storynory.com.

ST PATRICK'S DAY

Aim
To learn about how St Patrick became the patron saint of Ireland and how St Patrick's Day is celebrated today.

Preparation
Prepare to play 'St Patrick's Day Song', which is available on YouTube. Other songs with which pupils could join in and sing include 'I'm a Little Leprechaun' by The Kiboomers and 'Oh Danny Boy'. You could also prepare some traditional songs, such as 'Galway Bay' and 'My Wild Irish Rose', to play as they enter the hall.

Make copies of the St Patrick's Day assembly script which is available from www.primaryresources.co.uk, and ask a year 5 class to prepare a presentation in which they either act out or read the script.

Invite a group of children to dress up as leprechauns and prepare a leprechaun dance.

Introduction
Explain that very little is known about St Patrick's life except that he is credited with introducing Christianity to Ireland in the fifth century AD. He became the patron saint of Ireland, and St Patrick's Day is celebrated on March 17 in Ireland, the USA and other countries around the world.

Main focus: The story of St Patrick
Invite the year 5 class to present the story of St Patrick which they have prepared.

Then play the video of the St Patrick Day Song.

Conclusion
End with a performance of the leprechauns' dance.

Thought for the day

St Patrick's Day toasts:

> May the roof above us never fall in and may the friends beneath remain friends for ever.

> May your blessings outnumber
> The shamrocks that grow
> And may trouble avoid you
> Wherever you go.

Further resources

A scripted assembly telling the story of how St Patrick drove all the snakes out of Ireland is available from the Assembly Box website.

A video telling the story of St Patrick that is suitable for infants can be found at www.bbc.co.uk/cbeebies/watch/lets-celebrate-st-patricks-day.

A PowerPoint presenting what we know of St Patrick's life is available from www.slideshare.net.

WORLD BOOK DAY

World Book Day is celebrated on different days in different countries. This assembly can be used whenever World Book Day is being celebrated.

Aim

To understand the important part that books have played in the development of ideas and how books can be a source of enjoyment as well as knowledge.

Preparation

Make a copy of the poem 'The Secrets Box' to put on the whiteboard.

Collect a variety of different books from the library – a fiction book, an information book, a dictionary, a poetry book, a bible, a book of jokes.

Ask each of the children in their classes to write down the title and author of their favourite book, and to think about why they like the book; e.g. is it funny or exciting? Get them to choose a short passage from the book which they particularly like, and to read it to a partner and say why they chose that passage and why they like the book.

Introduction

Explain that World Book Day is held on different days in different countries. It is usually held in March in the UK.

Read this poem:

The Secrets Box
> These are the keys
> That open the locks
> Of the secrets box.
>
> This is the secrets box
> Where deep inside
> The stories hide.
>
> This is the girl
> Who found the keys
> That open the locks
> Of the secrets box.
>
> These are the stories
> Of dragons and kings.
> Of wizards and rings,
> Of dancing and sighs,
> Of sunshine and lies
> That are waiting within
> The secrets box.
>
> This is the girl
> Who read the stories
> That lay inside
> And laughed and cried.

Ask: What is the secrets box? What does the poem say about reading and stories?

Main focus: Why are books important?

Ask: Why do we read? Talk about reading in order to discover new facts, to check facts, to think about ideas and about reading for pleasure – reading stories that take us to new worlds and introduce us to how other people think and feel.

Explain that there are many kinds of books and ask: What different types of books are there?

Hold up examples of the different types of book that you have collected from the library and talk about each type. Ask: Which type of book do you think has had most influence on the way we live?

Point out the influence that holy books such as the Guru Granth Sahib, the Bible and the Koran have had on people's lives and how books of political ideas have had a great impact, such as those by Karl Marx and Mao Tse Tung.

Conclusion

End with the thought for the day.

Thought for the day

There is more treasure in books than in all the pirate's loot on Treasure Island.

Walt Disney

Further resources

Details of authors who can be invited to visit the school and take part in the assembly can be found at www.authorsalouduk.co.uk and www.contactanauthor.co.uk.

Appendix

Alphabetical list of topics

Anger
Bullying
Chinese New Year
Christmas
Endangered species
Divali
Eid-al-Fitr
Eid-al-Adha
Exercise
Greed
Guru Nanak's Birthday
Happiness
Harvest
Healthy Eating
Manners
National Pet Day
Perseverance
Right and Wrong
Rights and Responsibilities
Rules
Sadness
Safer Internet Day
Safety at home
Safety in the Street
Safety on the Road
Saint Andrew's Day
Saint David's Day
Saint George's Day
Saint Patrick's Day
Saying Sorry

Tolerance
World Book Day
World Forests Day
World Homeless Day
World Hunger Day
World Oceans Day
World Peace Day
World Recycling Day
Zoo Awareness Day

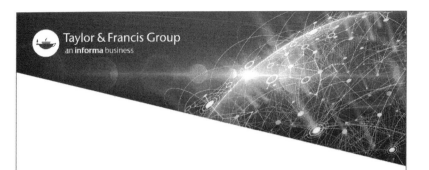

Printed in Great Britain
by Amazon

21030959R00077